Opera
Guide

Siegfried
Wagner

Lauritz Melchior as Siegfried (Royal Opera House Archives)

Preface

This series, published under the auspices of English National Opera and The Royal Opera, aims to prepare audiences to enjoy and evaluate opera performances. Each book is the product of many hands. The Guides to *The Ring of the Nibelung* contain Wagner's text and the translation by Andrew Porter, with a list of musical leitmotifs. The accompanying essays have been commissioned to give an insight into each work, as well as a perspective on the cycle as a whole.

ENO is most grateful to National Westminster Bank for sponsoring *The Ring* Guides, as well as the new production of the cycle. This sponsorship which has already supported Opera Guides and productions of *Fidelio* and *The Mastersingers of Nuremberg* forms part of the Bank's wide-ranging programme of community service.

Nicholas John
Series Editor

Siegfried

Richard Wagner

Opera Guide Series Editor: Nicholas John

Published in association with
English National Opera and The Royal Opera
This Guide is sponsored by ♻ **National Westminster Bank**

 John Calder · London
Riverrun Press · New York

First published in Great Britain, 1984 by
John Calder (Publishers) Ltd, 18 Brewer Street,
London W1R 4AS

and

First published in the U.S.A., 1984, by
Riverrun Press Inc,
175 Fifth Avenue
New York, NY 10010

BRITISH LIBRARY CATALOGUING IN PUBLICATION DATA
Wagner, Richard, *1813-1883*
 Siegfried.—(Opera guide; 28)
 1. Wagner, Richard, *1813-1883*   Siegfried
 2. Operas—Librettos
 I. Title   II. John, Nicholas   III. Series
 782.1'092'4   ML410.W15

LIBRARY OF CONGRESS CATALOGING IN PUBLICATION DATA
Wagner, Richard, 1813-1883
 [Ring des Nibelungen. Siegfred. Libretto. English & German]
 Siegfried.

 (Opera guide; 28)
 Includes index
 Discography: p. 126
 Bibliography: p. 127
 1. Operas—Librettos.   I. Title   II. Series.
 ML50.W14R62 1984   84-755657
 ISBN 0-7145-4040-4

SUBSIDISED BY THE
Arts Council
OF GREAT BRITAIN

John Calder (Publishers) Ltd, English National Opera and
The Royal Opera House, Covent Garden Ltd receive financial
assistance from the Arts Council of Great Britain. English
National Opera also receives financial assistance from the
Greater London Council.

Typeset in Plantin by Margaret Spooner Typesetting, Dorchester, Dorset.

Printed in Great Britain by The Alden Press, Oxford.

Contents

List of Illustrations

Educating Siegfried

Ulrich Weisstein

'A born anarchist, the ideal of Bakoonin.'
  G.B. Shaw, *The Perfect Wagnerite*[1]
'A regular L'il Abner type.'
  Anna Russell, '*The Ring of the Nibelung*, An Analysis'[2]

Contrary to Wagner's sure hopes and certain expectations,[3] *Siegfried*, the third instalment of *The Ring*, is the least popular and least frequently performed part of the tetralogy, even though it is chock-full of ingratiating musical numbers, such as Mime's lullaby, the forging song, *Forest Murmurs*, horn calls, real and imitated bird song, and the glorious duet at its conclusion. And the comedienne, Anna Russell, speaking for those who regard Wotan's scenes with Mime and Erda as tedious stretches of conversation which repeat information already familiar from *The Rhinegold* and *The Valkyrie*, in her plot summary undertaken from the perspective of the 'average opera-goer', dismisses this 'heroic *opéra-comique*'[4] by observing: 'There is not much you need to know about [it] except that Wotan comes down and plays "Twenty Questions".' The work is, however, pivotal to the action of the cycle and offers vital insights into Wagner's overall conception. For Siegfried is, like Gottfried von Strassburg's Parsifal, the *tumbe Tor* (the ignorant fool), and it is he who, with Brünnhilde, is destined to lay the foundation for a new world unencumbered by brute force (the giants), cunning (the dwarfs) and legal power upheld by contracts (Wotan). This part of the cycle thus sets the stage for *Twilight of the Gods* (*Götterdämmerung*), an anarchist's dream of total destruction which paves the way for a new order of things.

Unlike the scores of *The Ring* (originally *Der Reif des Nibelungen*, i.e. *The Circlet of the Nibelung*), which were written in the order of the dramatic action between 1853 and 1874, with a seven-year break for *Tristan and Isolde* and *The Mastersingers of Nuremberg*[5], the texts were produced in reverse order, from *Twilight of the Gods* (originally *Siegfried's Death*, 1848) by way of *Siegfried* (originally *Young Siegfried*, 1851) backwards to *The Valkyrie* (June, 1852) and *The Rhinegold* (originally *The Theft of the Rhinegold*, mid-September to early November, 1852), because Wagner felt the need to work out the action in a fully realised visual concept[6]. After major revisions of *Siegfried's Death* and relatively minor surgery on *Young Siegfried*, the first integral version of the poem was printed in February, 1853, in a private edition of fifty copies. Following further cosmetic changes, primarily affecting Parts Three and Four, the final draft of the cycle appeared, at long last, in 1863, thirteen years before the quadruple première in Bayreuth. Thus the text of each unit of *The Ring* evolved, by way of extrapolation, from narrative passages in the one chronologically preceding it: the action of *Siegfried* was derived from the hero's retrospective account in Act Three, Scene Two, of *Siegfried's Death*[7], just as that of *The Valkyrie* originated in Brünnhilde's report in Act Three of *Young Siegfried*[8]. Wagner discarded that report when he gave *Siegfried* its final form; but Siegfried's narrative, though modified and slightly abridged, is retained in *Twilight of*

Max Alvary (1856-1898) as Siegfried (The Royal College of Music)

the Gods. Although the scenes in which previous events are recapitulated may at first seem redundant to audiences attending the whole cycle, Wagner considered them intrinsic to his overall plan. Each of Wotan's question-and-answer sessions in *Siegfried*, for example, offers a new interpretation of the crucial incidents of the myth and consequently builds up for us a terrifying picture of the complex forces in Wotan's world. It is this world into which Siegfried, the Wälsung hero, ignorantly blunders.

Structurally, *Siegfried*, a veritable tragi-comedy,[9] is peculiar in so far as it consists of two interlarded sets of scenes, those concerned with Siegfried and those dominated by the Wanderer (i.e. Wotan in disguise). Originally, this drama exclusively focussed on the overgrown boy-scout (Ernest Newman's label for Siegfried), and the action, accordingly, was more or less straightforward comedy, first farcical and then sublime. There is no reference to the Father of the Gods in the relevant section of the original outline, *The Nibelung Myth as Sketch for a Drama* (1848); nor does he figure in *Siegfried's Death*. Wotan makes his grand entrance only in the prose sketch for *Young Siegfried* (early May, 1851), where we are told of an encounter with the dwarf: 'The [Wanderer] comes. Conversation while Mime works at his forge. The origin of the Nibelungs, etc.'. In the prose version, finished in late May of the same year, his role is considerably expanded and the dialogue with Mime augmented by conversations with Erda and Siegfried (Act Three), to which the verbal exchange with Alberich (and, briefly, Fafner) was subsequently added in lieu of a scene featuring the Nibelung hordes.

Wagner's reasons for enlarging Wotan's role are obvious: he needed to integrate Siegfried's *comédie humaine* with the remainder of *The Ring* and to juxtapose his hero's antics with the metaphysical drama of the rest of the cycle. This was done at the expense of stylistic unity and theatrical effectiveness, except in the truly Sophoclean confrontation between father and son in Act Three, where the two strands of the action overlap as Wotan vainly seeks to bar Siegfried's way. (In the draft, Wagner permitted the Wanderer to let the youth pass without a struggle; but in the final version the scene ends with the shattering of Wotan's spear by Siegmund's reconstituted sword — a parallel in reverse of the conclusion of Act Two of *The Valkyrie*, where it was the sword that was shattered by the spear.) For Wotan's scenes, in which the power structure of the universe is described, (scenes according to Anna Russell of 'crashing boredom' especially when Erda the 'green-faced torso' is involved) Wagner adopts rhetorical devices very different from the sprightly character of the scenes which highlight Siegfried's boisterous apprenticeship — his *Lehrjahre* — under the tutelage of a misshapen pedagogue.[10] It is on these that we shall concentrate. To appreciate the results of Siegfried's upbringing in the backwoods, it is useful to know something about his teacher, and before scrutinizing Mime's unorthodox educational methods, we shall do well to draw a portrait of this guardian who justifiably presents himself to his ward as midwife, nurse, father and mother rolled into one. Our understanding of the standard text will be greatly enhanced by tracing the evolution of certain significant traits, especially the change of tone from serious to mock-heroic. In *The Nibelung Myth as Sketch for a Drama*, Mime is still conceived as a person worthy of his calling, a veritable Chiron to his Siegfried/Achilles. The following epitome of what would have been Act One of *Siegfried* shows him to be well-meaning and supportive:

> After a long pregnancy, the cast-out Sieglinde gives birth to Siegfried in the Wilderness ... Reigin (Mime), Alberich's brother, emerged from clefts in the rock when she cried out in her birth-pangs and lent her a helping hand. Shortly after having given birth to Siegfried, Sieglinde dies, after telling Reigin her story and entrusting the boy to him. Reigin brings Siegfried up, informs him of his father's death, teaches him how to forge metal and procures the two pieces of his father's splintered sword, out of which, under his direction, Siegfried fashions Balmung (= Notung).

Max Lorenz as Siegfried (Royal Opera House Archives)

Ernst Kraus as Siegfried in Berlin (BBC Hulton Picture Library)

Up to this point, Mime's portrait is altogether positive. The catch, which in the final poem is manifest from the beginning, is revealed only in a subsequent passage:

> Now Mime incites the youth to kill the worm, in order to show his gratitude. Siegfried first wishes to avenge his father's death. He leaves the cave [. . .] and kills Hunding. Only after having done so, he fights and kills the dragon. When he puts his fingers, which are hot from the worm's blood, to his mouth in order to cool them, he involuntarily tastes the blood and in this way suddenly understands the language of the forest birds [here still in the plural] . . . They praise his deed . . . and warn him of Mime, who, they say, has used him only to get to the treasure and now craves his life in order to win the treasure for himself.[11]

The complimentary image of Mime as skilled artisan and devoted teacher is not only retained but strengthened in *Siegfried's Death*, where the hero, no longer the Innocent Abroad but still essentially without gall or guile, recalls his childhood from the perspective of the trusting ward. In the prose version of the *proto-Twilight of the Gods*, for example, his hunchback foster-father is

10

called a strong dwarf, splendid smith, and wise counsellor; and in the metrical version he appears, with alliterative force, as a manly creature, excellent smith and prudent counsellor to the orphaned boy.[12]

By the time Wagner set out to write *Young Siegfried*, Mime's character had changed for the worse, and the well-intentioned craftsman/philosopher/pedagogue had turned into a bundle of ill-assorted and unsavoury features. In both versions of *Siegfried* he shows himself to be a windbag, hypocrite, liar, weakling and coward. The fact that Mime, the clownish mimic, does not honour the truth is repeatedly demonstrated, although some of the apparent contradictions between the truth and his deceptive representation of it can be resolved by a comparison between the texts of *Siegfried* and *Young Siegfried*, which shows that Wagner was not uniformly successful in eliminating discrepancies.[13]

Thus, in an aside during his verbal sparring with Wotan in the first act of *Siegfried*, Mime admits having stolen the pieces of Siegmund's sword which in Act Three of *The Valkyrie*, Brünnhilde had handed over to Sieglinde: 'Cursed steel, / that I stole you!', thereby contradicting the evidence he himself had recently provided to Siegfried: 'This your mother gave me. / For labour, food and service / it was my wretched wage. / Look here, a broken sword! / She said your father bore it / when he died in his last fight'.[14] There are two ways of interpreting this passage: either Mime is deliberately misrepresenting the facts in order not to arouse Siegfried's suspicion or, as Newman considers to be more likely, Wagner simply overlooked the discrepancy.[15]

That Mime is insidious and hides his dubious purposes under a torrent of deceitful phrases is made explicit when Siegfried, coached by the little Woodbird, learns to distinguish between essence and appearance. The comic dialogue in Act Two, where, much against his will ('I didn't say that. / You get me all wrong'), Mime is forced to speak the truth — a device purportedly borrowed from a nineteenth-century Faust play — offers irrefutable proof of his duplicity.[16]

Ticho Parly as Siegfried at Covent Garden in 1967 (photo: Reg Wilson)

Heinrich Gudehus (1845-1909) as Siegfried. He was Covent Garden's first Tristan and Walther von Stolzing. (The Royal College of Music)

As a weakling, the Mime of *Siegfried* is no longer fit to assist the protagonist in remaking his father's weapon but is reduced to playing the role of an onlooker. Admitting his own inferiority as a craftsman, he decides to change his profession and with mordant black humour exchanges the smith's apron for the cook's: 'When the master finds his skill has gone, / he serves as cook to the child. / If he makes a paste from the steel, / I shall brew him / a broth out of eggs.' A picture of cowardice, he spends much of his time quaking in his boots, crouching behind the anvil or hiding in a corner, whether in response to Siegfried's roughhousing (in the episode with the bear), Wotan's threatening gesture with the spear, or the waking nightmare of Fafner's arrival. How ironic, and yet how appropriate, that it is he who should offer to give lessons in fear!

Turning to Siegfried, we note that in his physical and psychological makeup he combines traits derived from heroic legend (*Sage*) and fairy tale (*Märchen*). As a slayer of patently allegorical dragons ('Here I rest and possess', says Fafner, the perfect capitalist) he is quite at home in the heroic legend, and as the Youth Who Knew No Fear of fairy tale, he would seem to have no place in the weighty mythological context of *The Ring* — not so, however, according to Wagner. For in a conversation with the sculptor Gustav Kietz, in 1849, the composer programmatically stated: 'I shall write no more Grand Operas. I shall write fairy tales, like the one about the Youth Who Went Forth to Learn What Fear Was.'[17] Wagner had fallen in love with this idea. Having completed the prose sketch for *Young Siegfried*, he told his friend Theodor Uhlig of the discovery which, striking him with the force of inspiration, had enabled him to graft one genre upon the other:

> All winter long I have been haunted by an idea which, quite recently, has so completely captivated me that I shall now bring it to fruition. Didn't I tell you, some time ago, about a humorous subject, i.e., the story of the fellow who sets out to learn what fear is but cannot bring himself to do so? Consider my surprise when suddenly I realized that that fellow is none other than — the young Siegfried who acquires the treasure and awakens Brünnhilde.[18]

Almost concurrently it dawned on him that placing the folktale before the legend/myth — the *Ring* being then conceived as a mere diptych — would permit him, in line with the Horatian formula *utile dulci* (i.e. both instructive and entertaining), to ease his audience into the high tragic mode: '*Young Siegfried* offers the enormous advantage of acquainting the audience with the weighty myth in a playful manner, just as the fairy tale does with children. Everything is engraved upon the mind by distinct, sensuous impressions; everything is understood — and when the serious *Siegfried's Death* arrives the audience knows everything that is presupposed there or could only be hinted at, and I've won the game.'

Let us now trace the development of the text of the scenes which deal with Siegfried's acquisition of knowledge and experience. Wagner had considerable difficulty making 'ends meet' in this particular instance. If, once again, we search for evidence in the original plot outline of *The Ring*, *The Nibelung Myth as Sketch for a Drama*, we find that, at that point, Wagner had not yet linked fairy story and heroic legend, although even then he must have known that in the Teutonic legends Siegfried is commonly referred to as one who knows no fear, which, naturally, is a far cry from saying that, for whatever reasons, he must learn it.

The question of fear (*Furcht*) — whose existential analogue is anguish (*Angst*), a notion which is introduced at a much later stage in Act Three with reference to Sieglinde and Brünnhilde — is first raised in the prose sketch for *Young Siegfried*. The motivation furnished in this context is extremely poor, however, for it is Siegfried himself who broaches the subject 'out of the blue'. Asked by his tutor what he would do once Mime had mended the sword, the pupil emphatically states: 'That I have told you long ago. Into the world will I fare and learn fearing since I will never learn it from you.' Surely, this explanation is unsatisfactory since we cannot be certain when and under what circumstances the notion popped into Siegfried's head or whether Mime planted it there to begin with. Wagner must have noticed that this was a grave lacuna and, resolving the issue in his mind, added a note which supplies the much needed rhyme and reason:

> Siegfried now feels himself quite free of Mime. He will leave him in order to go into the world: for this reason he once more demands the sword. Mime tries to instil into him fear of the world so as to keep him in the wood. He paints for him one terror after another in the world beyond the wood. . . . Argument over fearing. Mime must explain it. He describes fear. Siegfried cannot learn it and now will go forth just to learn it. (Mime resolves quickly to teach it to him *himself*. Fafner? . . .)

In the corresponding passage of *Young Siegfried*, Wagner realizes this idea but unduly complicates matters by coupling the notion of fear with that of cunning (*List*). Here Mime acquaints his ward with what he claims to be the educational policy framed by his mother on her deathbed: 'Mime . . ., / you clever man! / When my child grows up one day / keep the courageous one in the wood! / The world is malicious and false; / it sets traps for the simpleton. /

*Ernestine Schumann-Heink as
Erda, Wilhelm Gruning as
Siegfried and Hans Breuer as Mime
at Bayreuth in 1897
(Royal Opera House Archives)*

Only he who has learned fear / may keep himself tolerably safe.'[19] Whereupon the impetuous Siegfried expresses his wish to acquire fear. Mime will teach it to him (or so he thinks) together with its antidote *List*: 'It is cunning / which fear teaches us. / It is the fruit of fear.' On second thought, while working on the final version of the text, Wagner must have observed that, from the dwarf's point of view, such instruction would be counterproductive; for if Mime succeeded in teaching Siegfried cunning he would quickly be up to his teacher's tricks.

Accordingly, in the text that finally emerged and served as a basis for the composition of the music Mime does not teach Siegfried anything (except speech, and even that reluctantly[20]). As for cunning, it is the Woodbird which introduces him, with Fafner's posthumous help, to the art of double hearing, which enables him to cope with Mime's double talk in what may be the most amusing scene in all of *The Ring*:

MIME:	Siegfried, my son,
	you see it yourself:
	you will have to yield your life to me.
SIEGFRIED:	That you hate me
	I am pleased to hear,
	but must I yield my life as well?
MIME:	That's not what I said.
	You get me all wrong.

Although the intrinsic motif of fear was retained, it was altered from phase to phase of the creative process. Thus both in *Young Siegfried* and in *Siegfried* it is neither the protagonist nor Mime but the Wanderer who brings up the subject, and each time in a different manner. In the *Ur*-libretto Wotan insinuates to Mime that it is his own disciple who will slay him

15

('Only Siegfried himself / can forge his sword. / Your clever head / keep for yourself; / I do not need useless things. / But take good care of it / from now on!'); but the dwarf, blind for all his shrewdness, fails to put two and two together. In *Siegfried*, on the other hand, Wotan, linking the forging of the sword with the acquisition of fear and embedding both motifs in a riddle, prophesies: 'Now, Fafner's dauntless destroyer, / hear, you doomed dwarf: / "Only he who has never / learned to fear / will fashion Notung anew." / Your wise head / guard in future; / I leave it forfeit to him / who has not learned to fear.'

Much against his better knowledge, which he seeks desperately to suppress, Mime himself tries to piece Notung together but quickly realizes that the task is beyond him and that, accordingly, his life is doomed ('My wise head / I have lost in the wager. / Doomed, I lost it to him / who has not learned to fear'); but at this point he still fails to identify his slayer as Siegfried. That is the next step, for once Siegfried, has done the seemingly impossible by forging Notung, there can be no doubt as to who will kill him. It is then that he decides on a new course of action, namely that of instilling fear in the youth, since, according to Wotan's prophecy, one who has learned to fear cannot be Mime's murderer. Yet, on second thought he realizes that he is now caught on the horns of a dilemma: if things are to work out as he wants, Siegfried must forge the sword and dispatch the dragon but, having been struck with fear in the process, must then meet his own fate:

> How do I hide
> my anxious head?
> It is forfeited to the bold youth
> unless Fafner teaches him fear.
> But woe, poor me!
> How could he wring the worm's neck
> if it taught him to fear?
> How would I attain the ring?
> Darned fix!
> I would be stuck
> if I didn't find a way
> to subdue the fearless one.[21]

Since the scenario that would suit Mime best — Siegfried killing Fafner and, in turn, being killed by him — is unlikely to be enacted, the resourceful dwarf literally concocts an alternate plan: he will cook a poisonous broth (*Sudel*), which he will dish up to the thirsty boy after the fight. The plan backfires, and Siegfried emerges unscathed but without having learnt to fear. Still uncertain of his calling but acting on another hint from the Woodbird, he embarks on a new adventure beyond the *selva oscura*, the dark wood of ignorance and sexual innocence in which Mime has raised him.

Having, still fearless, pierced the wall of flames, he meets his Beatrice, Brünnhilde, whom at first he mistakes for his mother. In her realm he is to acquire his sentimental education. What he is to learn now is a kind of fear that is in no way physical. Rather he, the loner, who has until now met only animals, dwarfs, giants and gods, is to become a thinking and feeling member of the human race. Face to face with the woman (of divine origin) who is to initiate him into love, he is consumed by the very fear which he is 'burning' to possess. Approaching the sleeping Valkyrie, he reflects:

> How do I, coward, feel?

Jean de Reszké as Siegfried in 1896 (Royal Opera House Archives)

Is this what fear is?
O mother! mother!
Your brave child!
There's a woman asleep
who taught him fear.
How conquer fear?
How muster courage?
To awake myself
I must awaken the maiden.

Fear it is, but of an entirely different order. In the words of Patrick McCreless, 'Siegfried is involved with two very different kinds of fear: physical fear, or fear of death, and the perfectly valid emotional fear which is the basis of sensitivity to other human beings and underlies human relationships. Although the two seem to be equated in the drama — they are in no way differentiated in the text — the story simply does not make sense if there is no distinction drawn between them'. This is exactly the point and, accordingly, the progression from physical fear to emotional fear signals genuine progress. This different type of fear is the first step in his experience of human love, which in turn gives him back the confidence to forget self-doubt. Indeed, as soon as he has discovered what it feels like to be afraid in an emotional sense he also learns that another new experience, that of human love, enables him to overcome it.

As the fire in the blood is kindled,
as we pierce each other with our glances,
as we burn in ardent embraces,
my keen courage
returns to me,
and the fear, ah!
which I never learned,
the fear which you
taught me just now:
that fear, it seems,
fool that I am,
I forgot altogether.

Unlike the boy in the Grimm Brothers' fairy tale who, having passed through his ordeals with flying colours, finally gets his wish when a waiting-maid dumps a bucket of gudgeons over his head, Siegfried, having been gripped by fear on the threshold of his humanity, quickly unlearns it. Love, united with knowledge and free of anguish, is about to conquer the world and, in the process, topple the mythological edifice erected in the earlier portions of *The Ring*. Like Pamina and Papageno in Mozart's *The Magic Flute*, Siegfried and Brünnhilde can dispense with heaven because love is heavenly: 'Mann und Weib und Weib und Mann / reichen an den Himmel an' ('Man and woman, and woman and man / reach up to heaven'). In gaining this insight, they have learned their lesson, and no further schooling is needed.

Notes

[1] The quotation is drawn from *The Works of Bernard Shaw* (London, 1930), XIX, 212.

[2] *The Anna Russell Album* published in 1972 by Columbia Masterworks.

[3] 'I am now convinced that as my most popular work *The Young Siegfried* will have a quick and happy dissemination and will pull along the other pieces, one by one, so that it will probably be the founder of a whole Nibelung dynasty.' Wagner in a letter to Julie Ritter dated May 6, 1857. This letter, as well as all other relevant statements by the composer, is culled from Richard Wagner, *Sämtliche Werke*, vol. 29/1: Dokumente zur Entstehungsgeschichte des Bühnenfestspiels *Der Ring des Nibelungen*, ed. W. Breig and H. Fladt (Mainz: Schott, 1976).

[4] Wagner uses that term in a letter to Hans Richter written in 1868, where it applies both to *Die Meistersinger* and *Siegfried*. In *Mein Leben* he calls it a 'heroic comedy'.

[5] The exact point of interruption is marked by a letter to Liszt dated June 28, 1857, where Wagner states: 'I have led my young Siegfried into the lonely beauty of the forest. There I have left him lying under the linden tree and have said farewell to him with heartfelt tears. There he is better off than elsewhere.'

[6] As Wagner points out in his autobiography, *Mein Leben*, it was the actor/director Eduard Devrient who, as early as 1848, demonstrated the need for a scenic, i.e. visual, realization of the entire story of the *Ring*. The first comprehensive outline of the tetralogy is sketched in letters to Uhlig (Nov. 12, 1851) and Liszt (Nov. 20, 1851).

[7] The full text of *Siegfrieds Tod* is found in vol. 6 of Wagner's *Gesammelte Schriften*, ed. J. Kapp (Leipzig, n.d. [1914]), 150-193.

[8] This text, like all other *Skizzen und Entwürfe zur Ring-Dichtung*, was edited by Otto Strobel (Munich, 1930). Relevant portions of *Der junge Siegfried* are reproduced in III, 315-333, of the Jubiläumsausgabe of the *Dichtungen und Schriften*, ed. D. Borchmeyer (Frankfurt, 1983).

[9] The generic question is raised in Patrick McCreless's *Wagner's 'Siegfried': Its Drama, History and Music* (Ann Arbor, 1982), to which I am greatly indebted.

[10] The Wanderer scene in Act One of *Siegfried* has been thoroughly analyzed by Reinhold Brinkmann in an essay published in 1972 in the *Jahrbuch des Staatlichen Instituts für Musikforschung Preussischer Kulturbesitz*.

[11] Siegfried's revenge on Hunding, which formed part of the action in the early versions, was finally eliminated by Wagner.

[12] 'Mime hiess ein mannlicher Zwerg. / Zirlich und scharf wusst' er zu schmieden. / Sieglind, meiner lieben Mutter, / half er im wilden Walde. / Den sie sterbend gebar, / mich Starken zog er auf / mit klugem Zwergenrat.'

[13] Daniel Coren compares the texts of the two versions in an unpublished dissertation 'A Study of Wagner's *Siegfried*' (Univ. of California, Berkeley, 1971).

[14] All quotations are based on Andrew Porter's English version (New York, 1977) but have been amended to make the text more literal for literary analysis.

[15] In general, the reader is alerted to Ernest Newman's subtle analysis in Chapter 17 ('Difficulties in the Rounding of the *Ring*') of vol. II of his *Life of Richard Wagner*.

[16] After an oral report recorded in Gustav Adolph Kietz's *Erinnerungen*.

[17] Here, too, the versions are at odds; for whereas in *Young Siegfried*, alerting the audience to things yet to pass, Wotan admonishes Mime to watch his tongue ('Hab' acht, wenn die Zunge dir schwankt, / Schwatze kein albernes Zeug!'), in *Siegfried* no such warning is sounded.

[18] The letter was written on May 10, 1851.

[19] In *Siegfried*, the corresponding passage reads: 'Your mother's counsel / speaks through me. / What I vowed / I must now fulfill: / not to dismiss you / into the cunning world / until you have learned how to fear.'

[20] This is evidenced in Act One, Scene One, where Siegfried, seizing Mime by the throat, violently complains: 'Then I must choke you / to learn anything; / of your own will / you tell me nothing. / Thus everything / I had to wrest from you. / I would hardly have learned / how to use speech / if I had not forced the scoundrel / to teach me.'

[22] Wagner deliberately couched the farcical passages of *Siegfried* in the colloquial language of low comedy. Thus 'darned fix' renders 'verfluchte Klemme' more closely than the 'accursed problem' of Andrew Porter's performing translation.

Donald McIntyre as the Wanderer and John Dobson as Mime in the production by Götz Friedrich at Covent Garden (photo: Reg Wilson)

'Siegfried': The Music

Anthony Newcomb

It is more accurate to speak of two *Siegfrieds* than of one *Siegfried*, at least as far as the music is concerned. The first consists of the first two acts of the opera, and was essentially completed in 1857, following some three years of sustained work on the music of the first two operas of *The Ring*.[1] The second consists of the last act, and was composed in 1869. The intervening dozen years had seen not only the composition of *Tristan*, the Paris revision of *Tannhäuser*, and *The Mastersingers*, but also the profound alteration in the external circumstances of Wagner's life caused by the intervention of King Ludwig of Bavaria and by his marriage to Cosima von Bülow. It is as if Dickens had returned to finish an incomplete *Nicholas Nickleby* after having finished *Bleak House*. A real, and even more extreme case in the visual arts is Michelangelo's completion of the back wall of the Sistine Chapel over 25 years after he had begun the project with the ceiling.

That being said, one must recognize the unity that holds the two *Siegfried*s together, making them one *Siegfried* after all. The most important force in creating this unity is not so much the plot, for the contrast between the rustic-comic, fairy-tale world of the first two acts and the exalted, epic flavour of the last act is pronounced. It is rather the network of musical motifs out of which all three acts are woven. To stop for some moments on this most distinctive aspect of Wagner's burgeoning musical technique will enable us to appreciate the consistent concerns that inform his evolution as musical dramatist during the 1850s and 1860s.

The concept of these motifs — named leitmotifs (German sing., *Leitmotiv*, pl., *Leitmotive*) by Wagner's amanuensis Hans von Wolzogen — is by no means the block-like, undifferentiated one it may seem. The simplest and most obvious form of musical recollection in opera, by no means an innovation with Wagner, is the repetition of entire phrases or sections of music, both as a form-building technique and as a dramatically suggestive device. Such a thing occurs, for instance, at the end of *The Rhinegold* with the repetition of the music for the entrance into Valhalla. What is repeated here is not a leitmotif, for it is not a motif. It is a section, built of several complete and coherent phrases. As such it is far too unwieldy for the kind of development and recombination by which Wagner wanted to weave the accompaniment of each new scene. The distinction between motif and phrase here is that between, on the one hand, the incomplete fragment and, on the other, the complete autonomous unit, with its own beginning, extension, and cadence. A leitmotif is a short, distinctive fragment of a phrase — perhaps just its first two measures, or even just its first or second measure — which is malleable enough for such ongoing developmental use. (See motif [8] for motivic extracts from the 'Valhalla' music.)

These motivic fragments are defined and identified by us according to a complex interaction of various musical elements, such as orchestration, rhythm, harmony, and melodic contour. In some, like the Valhalla motifs, all four elements are highly distinctive; in others, only two or three elements may be distinctive and memorable. As Wagner worked on the dramas of *The Ring* in 1853-57, he discovered that he could, by the abstraction of one or two

The stage setting for 'Siegfried' Act One at Bayreuth, 1901 (BBC Hulton Picture Library)

distinctive elements of a motif from the others, unlock rich musical possibilities, both for combination of old motifs and for development of new.

For example, Wagner's motivic combinations are often more complicated and subtler than just the simultaneous, contrapuntal restatement of two pre-existent motifs. By combining, let us say, the melodic contours and rhythmic shape of one motif with the harmonic changes of another, and overlaying the whole with a distinctive short figure extracted from yet another, one creates both a complicated new texture, in purely musical terms, and a psychologically complex musical reference. An example that leaps immediately to mind is the combination thus made of the motifs of the Ride of the Valkyries (motif 35), of Wotan's dejection (motif 36b), of the Treaty (motif 9a), and of the Downfall of the Gods (motifs 24 and 25 in succession) in the Prelude to the third act of *Siegfried*. Often, by just altering an orchestral colour or a rhythmic detail in one motif, Wagner can effect such a combination with another, suggesting connections between psychological worlds that had previously seemed distinctly separate.

Similarly, by the abstraction of individual musical elements from various previous motifs and their combination with new elements, Wagner can develop motifs that are new but not entirely so — transforming some elements of previous motifs into new motifs that are tied to a particular past, and that announce their lineage in a series of distinctive family features. Thus Wotan, when he first appears as the Wanderer in *Siegfried*, enters to a wonderfully distinctive series of chords (motif 49a) that retains, in its rhythmic style and its chromatic harmonic style, a connection with his most recent past action, the casting of the spell over Brünnhilde (motif 42). Again,

Illustration from 'The Sphere' on May 10, 1913 of Peter Cornelius as Siegfried and Minnie Saltzmann-Stevens as Brünnhilde in Act Three (Royal Opera House Archives)

the psychological implications of these family lineages — of the pedigree of each new motif or theme — can be considerable. Wagner had mastered this idea as early as the interlude between the first and second scenes of *The Rhinegold*, when he evolved the Valhalla motif [8] from the Ring motif [6] by keeping distinctive melodic and rhythmic features, while transforming them through changed orchestration and harmony. Thus the conceptual link between the seemingly disparate worlds of the Ring and Valhalla — a link fundamental to the entire cycle — is established immediately and in a way that could be done only with hundreds of words, and at the risk of tendentiousness.

Just as in their ways of combination and transformation, so in their ways of reference the leitmotifs are much more various than one might at first think. Few are connected simply and directly to an object, person, or situation, to which one can simply attach a word or phrase; most refer, from the moment of their first appearance, to the complex of emotions in a complex situation. Motifs [12] and [18], connected with the Giants and the Tarnhelm, provide as clear examples as any of the first kind of straightforward reference. Yet even these gain complexity of reference from what might be called musical metaphor, which goes beyond a label-like attachment through simultaneity of occurrence. For example, the Giants' motif, because of its slow, hammer-like rhythms and its melody of repeated notes and basic intervals, is a musical metaphor for blunt simple-minded strength. Similarly, the Tarnhelm motif, distinguished by its separate orchestral choir and strange modal harmonies, is a musical metaphor for strangeness and mystification, which connects it with the motif of the Potion that Siegfried drinks in *Twilight of the Gods*. Through

23

the operation of musical metaphor, the two motifs accompanying Siegmund and Sieglinde at their first appearance in the first scene of *The Valkyrie* (motifs 28 and 29), refer in a much more complex fashion than names. That both are fragile, single orchestral strands, defined only by an unassertive rhythmic shape and a gentle but distinctive melodic contour conveys the vulnerability and loneliness of the two young people. Siegmund's fatigue at this moment is conveyed by the slowly drooping shape of his motif [28], and by its slow beginning from a downbeat; to this are opposed the gentle rise and the upbeat metrical position of Sieglinde's motif [29], conveying her mild healing force. That the two are immediately combined, and fit so happily together as a contrapuntal combination of complementary tendencies already gives an idea of the destiny of the two characters.

It will be clear from a moment's theoretical thought (as it is from a few hours of listening to the operas themselves) that the possibilities opened up by such complex methods of reference, together with those offered by combining elements from various old motifs and by developing new ones along characteristic family lines, gave Wagner a ready means for a kind of running authorial commentary on the action of his dramas. We no longer have anything like a plot conveyed only by the dialogue and vocal and bodily gestures of the protagonists, as would be normal in drama. It may be more appropriate to think of his operas as musical novels than as musical dramas, because of the nearly constant, insistent presence of the more or less omniscient narrator-commentator.

One must remember at this point that the musical motifs of Wagner's operas do not exist solely to allow narrative commentary; they are also the stuff out of which the musical shapes are made. That is, they are not only illustrative, they are form-giving as well. The demands of these two functions do not always mesh smoothly, and Wagner resolved their often conflicting demands in various ways at various times as he worked on *The Ring*, even as he worked on the first two acts of *Siegfried*.

In approaching the topic of motivic usage in *Siegfried*, two considerations stand out: 1) the plot returns for the first time in the cycle to several characters that have not been in evidence since *The Rhinegold*; 2) as Wagner began work on *Siegfried*, he had not only over three years experience with his techniques, he also had, by Ernest Newman's count,[2] some 100 motifs to work with. As a result, the overture to the first act seems to announce a new importance for, and virtuosity in, motivic recombination. Instead of a relatively self-contained musical structure using only one or perhaps two closely related motifs — the kind of prelude we have heard before all previous acts of *The Ring* — we hear a loosely structured combination and concatenation of nearly ten distinct motifs from Scene Three of *The Rhinegold*, in particular those motifs connected with the Nibelungs Mime and Alberich. The music serves primarily to conjure up for us, without a word or a visual image, the relevant previous dramatic situation and state of mind. Even before the curtain goes up we realize that we have been made privy to Mime's brooding through a stream-of-consciousness-like series of brilliant musical illustrations. (Note, for example, shortly before the curtain, how Wagner gives Mime's vision of the broken sword, by changing the harmony and orchestration of its motif [27] while retaining its rhythm and melody.) In fact this brooding continues without interruption as the curtain goes up. Not until Siegfried's entrance is the continuity of the overture broken by the motif of youthful exuberance that will later become his horn call [45]. Mime's opening brooding is, in effect, a kind of accompanied recitative, whose unprecedentedly rich leitmotivic accompaniment is begun already by the prelude.

Once fairly underway, however, Act One as a whole recognizes the structuring power of song — of coherent phrase and section, as opposed to motif. Its first part (most of Scene One) is shaped by Mime's song about bringing up Siegfried, first complete, then interrupted in repetitions. Example 1 is the first phrase of the song, which Siegfried calls a 'Starenlied' i.e. a short, repetitive refrain.

The scene as a whole is formed by a loose alternation of this material of Mime's with Siegfried's own material: the horn call of motif [45] and, more insistently, motif [47], first announced when Siegfried impatiently shatters the sword that Mime has been working on. Wagner's new subtlety in the use of all aspects of leitmotif — not just initial motivic character, but evolution of that character as well — as a means of musical characterization governs the development of Siegfried's material in this scene. Thus Siegfried's first motifs are not, like Mime's, tuneful and well-structured; indeed, motif [47], the most used in this scene, is scattered, centrifugal, unfocussed in its intervals — another example of motivic meaning conveyed by musical metaphor. Mime's musical image is here in control; Siegfried's is energetic but not yet fully formed. His first step on the road to the maturity (albeit limited) that this act will bring him is the vigorous music that he sings just before storming out into the forest at the end of Scene One, wherein his impatient figure of motif [47] gets subordinated into the accompaniment (x in Example 2b below) of a now better formed, if still rather diffuse, snatch of tuneful song.

[2a]

SIEGFRIED

Aus dem Wald fort in die Welt zieh'n: nimmer kehr' ich zu-rück!

Through the wide world I shall wan-der, never-more to re-turn!

[2b]

SIEGFRIED

flieg' ich von hier, flu-the da-von,

so I shall fly float-ing a-far,

To skip for a moment over Scene Two, between Mime and the Wanderer, exactly this music returns when Siegfried rushes back in at the beginning of Scene Three. And as the scene progresses the previous musical roles of Siegfried and Mime are reversed. Mime's characteristic material is now the uncanny music of fear and trembling that surrounds him between the departure of the Wanderer at the end of Scene Two and the reappearance of Siegfried at the beginning of the next. This material, brilliantly colourful but unstructured, is as unable to impose order on the beginning of Scene Three as it is unable to convince Siegfried. It is finally Siegfried who shapes the end of the act by sweeping aside Mime's music and inventing a triumphant pair of songs of his own. He first makes the scalar descending fourths of the end of Example 2 (which will be the impetus for the music to Siegfried's Rhine journey in *Twilight of the Gods*) into a strongly shaped new tune, to which he fans the fire to the necessary heat for the forging of the sword.

[3]

SIEGFRIED
Belebt

Then he manages finally to focus the tremendous, athletic energy of motif 47 around a single pitch centre and hammer it into a new, powerfully repetitive and clearly structured four-measure phrase, the basis of the song to which he forges the sword itself.

[4]

Heavy and strong, not too fast

In this, the last song of this act of songs, even the internal structure is clear. After a first stanza with its own clearly defined beginning, middle, and cadential sections, Siegfried brushes aside the brief interjection of Mime and repeats the music literally for a second stanza — an almost unheard-of procedure in Wagner's mature style. The directness of this form is again a musical metaphor for Siegfried's finding his own direction.

Eva Turner as Brünnhilde in Turin, 1933 (Royal Opera House Archives)

Siegfried's two songs are the form-giving thematic elements in Scene Three, just as Mime's was in Scene One. Because of their length, and their strong internal structure and coherence, they are not leitmotifs, though they can and will be fragmented into motivic material. (Motif 51, for example, is extracted from a later stanza of the song in Example 3.) Song, made up of clearly shaped, coherent phrases on the one hand, and motif, or brief malleable fragment on the other, go together to form the thematic material of Wagner's music dramas.[3] In *Siegfried*, Wagner is getting increasingly flexible and cunning in his ways of playing the two kinds of thematic material off one against the other, and of moving back and forth between them, for the purposes both of structure and of characterization.

The form-giving function in a scene is normally entrusted to some clearly shaped phrase or group of phrases, usually newly devised and stated near the outset. Where such a clear thematic shape is absent, music tends to be restricted to a purely illustrative function, commenting on a structure that is given by the text. Almost the first half of Act Two of *Siegfried* is like this: a triumph of the illustrative over the architectural function of motif and harmony. It is not until Siegfried relaxes under the linden tree and listens to the voices of the forest around him that the clear metrical and tonal structure of the forest music (motifs 53a-c) takes control first of the rest of the act, recurring like the main theme of an episodic rondo, and finally of Siegfried himself. There is a lot of scenic detail and action in this act as a whole, and Wagner glories in his new virtuosity at commentary by motivic transformation and combination. His motivic work, when combined with a brilliant orchestral writing that places unparalleled demands on the woodwinds and especially the brasses in order to paint some of the most detailed orchestral sound pictures ever conceived, creates colouristic music of a kind that would have left Wagner's predecessor Carl Maria von Weber dumb with admiration and wonder.

Indeed, one might hear the Wolfglen scene from *Der Freischütz* — a scene loved and admired by Wagner since childhood — as the model for much of this beginning of Act Two. To do so is to realize the tremendous leap taken by German Romantic opera in the intervening 35 years. The sense of the uncanny created in the Weber by the tritone-based tonal structure and by the omnipresence of Samiel's diminished-seventh chord (in fact a primitive leitmotif) is redoubled in the Wagner by a harmonic vocabulary so disorientated as to be almost atonal and by the omnipresent tritone motif of Fafner [52]. In both Weber and Wagner, the whole is made up of a succession of brilliant musical illustrations, loosely strung together and as various and as colourful as possible. The difference is that in the second act of *Siegfried*, virtuosity in the use of these techniques is carried to a point that no-one 35 years before — indeed, no-one 5 years before — would have thought possible.

Never again would Wagner let his structural sense be so inebriated by the illustrative power of orchestral colour and the leitmotif. The cause seems to have been the variety of stage action and scenic detail in the libretto at this point. One might at first think that a great deal of narrative reminiscence in a given scene would also call up a profusion of illustrative leitmotifs, thus overwhelming the structural function of thematic material. This seems to have been the case, for example, in Wotan's long narrative in Act Two, Scene Two of *The Valkyrie*. Yet in the Wanderer-Mime scene from Act One of *Siegfried*, Wagner shows that already in 1857 he could overcome such

Frida Leider as Brünnhilde in 1938 (Royal Opera House Archives)

difficulties, creating a scene that was at once rich with reflective narration and reminiscence, and clear in its overall dramatic and musical structure. And when he returned to compose Act Three, Scene One in 1869, he was able to take a similar but less clearly structured scene in the libretto and shape it through purely musical means into one of the strongest units of the entire *Ring*, thus proving that he had discovered in these scenes of narrative retrospection one of the richest veins of music-drama.

The Wanderer-Mime scene, placed as the contrasting middle section between two Siegfried scenes in the strong overall design of Act One, is perhaps the structural triumph of the early acts of *The Ring*. It also makes clear the particular advantages that accrue when librettist and composer are united in one person. In such a case, at the same time as the librettist designs his dramatic situations, he can also be weighing their possibilities as musical structures. Thus the demands of musical structure can influence the overall shape of the large dramatic structures from the moment of their conception, not just their details, *a posteriori*. Act One, Scene Two consists of two sets of three questions and answers, introduced, separated and concluded by three statements by the Wanderer. This dramatic shape seems almost conceived in musical forms. The framing statements easily become a quasi-architectural refrain, while the two sets of questions can be placed between the occurrences of the refrain, as a pair of free variation sets.

These formal structures give the scene a clear and readily understandable musical shape. Characterization, control of pacing, and the constantly evolving, kinetic quality that Wagner demanded in his musical forms can then be conveyed within both refrain and variations by manipulation of motif and of formal procedure. For example, the solemn self-assurance of the first set of questions, asked by Mime of the Wanderer, is conveyed by the

Amy Shuard as Brünnhilde at Covent Garden in 1967 (photo: Reg Wilson)

clear formal definition coming from a large repeated block of motifs, setting each of Mime's three questions and the beginning of each of the Wanderer's answers. Firmly located in this musical structure, the remainder of each of the Wanderer's answers is freed for non-structural motivic commentary, in illustration of the sizable retrospective narrations embodied in these answers. The second set of questions, which Mime must answer, varies this process in order to suggest the changing dramatic situation. That the form-defining repeated block of motivic material separating each answer starts out smaller here, and soon shrinks to nothing, means that there is in general less self-assurance, less almost ritualistic certainty conveyed. And the pauses for considered response between question and answer get smaller and smaller. This accelerated dramatic pacing, together with the erosion of formal clarity and motivic definition, suggest Mime's increasing lack of self-control, as he is consumed first by an uneasy, incredulous hope that he may be able to extricate himself from the situation, then by panic when he realizes that he cannot. Wagner reinforces this evolution by a gradual *accelerando* from the solemn pace of the Wanderer's refrain before the second set of questions to a frantic *presto* at the end of the last answer — a musical metaphor whose meaning undergoes an ironic twist at the end, since the fast tempo seems at first to reflect Mime's growing exhilaration and joy, but turns suddenly to a *presto* of panic at the end.

By the time of this last answer, both formal process and motivic material have become ill-defined and centrifugal (Mime turns finally to the scattered energy of motif [47]). The Wanderer then brings the formal process back under control with a gesture whose effortless mastery comes not from the illustrative but from the structural function of motif. Stated in the simplest formal terms, he returns to the refrain of his beginning and middle

Alberich (Malcolm Rivers) quarrels with Mime (Paul Crook) at ENO, 1976 (photo: John Garner)

statements, imposing a sudden calm on the music and rounding off a formal process that seemed to be about to run out of control. This refrain, however, is itself formally quite complicated, and undergoes across the scene an evolution similar to that in the question-answer sets, and one that sets up the final musico-dramatic effect.

Upon the Wanderer's entrance at the beginning of the scene the refrain is stated complete, as the form-giving element in the scene. It is quite long, and structured rather like a Baroque ritornello, with a striking opening phrase [49a], more relaxed, sequential internal phrases [49b and c], and a cadential phrase. After this opening statement, it is never again repeated complete. First it is repeated to fix its main phrases in our memory, but without its short cadential phrase, which allows it to flow directly into the continuation of the scene. From this point onward, the opening phrase of the refrain is not heard again in its original form. It is principally the later phrases of the refrain that are repeated and developed, interspersed with Mime's frightened, contrasting material, to form the opening portal of the scene. Likewise, the recurrence of the refrain between the two sets of questions avoids the complete opening phrase, using principally the later phrases in yet less stable variations, in order to reinforce the increasing instability of the dramatic situation. With this formal background, at the end of the scene Wagner needs only to bring back the striking initial phrase of the refrain, not heard since the beginning of the scene. With this single gesture, he can cap the flow of Mime's panic, express musically the Wanderer's calm sovereignty, and give a firm sense of regained control and closure to the scene. There is no need to repeat the entire large refrain, which would interrupt the forward flow of the drama and give the false impression that things were exactly where they had been at the beginning of the scene. The long-withheld opening phrase has in itself enough formal weight to round off the entire musico-dramatic structure.

The opening scene of Act Three uses a similar structure. The Wanderer enters and states at the outset a clearly shaped refrain that will serve as the principal structuring element in the scene. It is again a sizable self-contained unit made up of several smaller phrases, the principal of which is Example 5 (see also motif 55):

[5]

THE WANDERER

Dramatically the scene is, like Act One, Scene Two, a kind of dialogue, beginning as a question-answer exchange. As we have seen, this dramatic situation can fit easily into a kind of musical variation procedure, here alternating variations of the Wanderer's clearly formed, active song with variations of Erda's phlegmatic, passive motivic material (the slumber music of motif 42). With the overall formal and motivic process thus clearly defined, a quantity of other leitmotifs can enter in illustrative commentary to the questions and answers of the protagonists. Change in the formal process itself as it evolves then reinforces the dramatic evolution of the scene. As the scene progresses, the protagonists engage each other more closely in debate, and the solemn initial question-answer exchange becomes more heated. Erda gets angry, and the Wanderer's anger rises to meet hers. In the process, the motivically defined alternating variation procedure is eroded, and the clear formal process of the scene seems about to come entirely unhinged. As in the Wanderer-Mime scene, the structuring thematic material of both characters becomes increasingly fragmented, and the dramatic pacing is at the same time considerably accelerated. Finally the Wanderer, this time with a tremendous effort, recalls his initial refrain and transforms its motivic and harmonic shapes into the grandiose new motif [56] by which he willingly renounces his power and proclaims Siegfried's inheritance.[4]

Walter Widdop as Siegfried at Covent Garden in 1935 (Royal Opera House Archives)

Particularly striking in comparing these two externally similar scenes is not only the new motivic, contrapuntal, and referential density of the orchestral accompaniment, the fruit of a dozen years' growth as a musician, but also the complete abandonment of anything like recitative. While large sections of Acts One and Two seemed accompanied recitative writ large, wherein a rather formulaic and shapeless vocal line was supported sometimes by simple chords, sometimes by a discontinuous quilt of leitmotivic commentary, Wagner in Act Three, Scene One gives every vocal line coherence and shape, and never lets the orchestral accompaniment subside into a shapeless patchwork of pre-existent motifs. The talky kind of passage that begins both sets of questions in the Wanderer-Mime scene, where the forward direction reverts entirely to the text, has disappeared entirely. In its place is a highly continuous orchestral polyphony (what Wagner in *The Music of the Future* of 1860 had termed *unendliche Melodie*) supporting a heightened kind of speech song, whose intensity sometimes brings it close to Schoenberg's experiments 50 years later.

That Wagner had consciously rejected the model of recitative is indicated by a passage of March 12 1869 from Cosima Wagner's diary: 'At tea he said that, if he wanted to make things easy for himself, he would, from the moment Wotan says, 'Seit mein Wunsch es will' ('I have willed that end!') [where he now sings the first phrase of the recapitulated refrain], introduce recitative, which would certainly create a great effect, but would put an end to the work as art. Nobody has yet noticed with how much art he has employed all means to prevent the interruption of the flow of melody . . .'[5] That Wagner struggled over this moment in the scene more than was his wont is shown both by entries in Cosima's diary (June 28, July

3, July 7) to the effect that he was still working on it long after his sketching in general had progressed to the third scene of the act, and by the surviving first draft, which has a page cut out of it and replaced at this point. Wagner's final solution provides for both the declamatory freedom of recitative and the form-giving power of the clearly shaped phrase. Wotan announces his momentous decision to Erda over the first phrase of his refrain, but each successive chord of the refrain is held in suspension, under written-out fermatas of varying lengths, while Wotan declaims freely over them.

A single example of the heightened speech-song of Wagner's late style will serve to illustrate how his vocal lines reveal, even exaggerate, the emotional state of his characters through the pitches and rhythms of their speech patterns. It can at the same time show the practical workings of Wagner's technique of poetry through alliteration and assonance, called *Stabreim*, and suggest some of the problems to be overcome in translating these librettos.

[6]

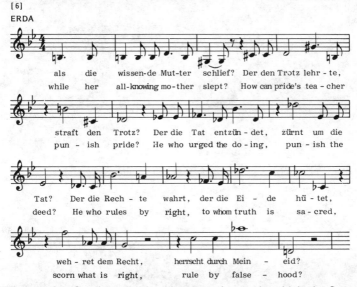

This is Erda's fourth speech in this scene, the one in which she first gets angry, and the point at which the dramatic pacing of the scene begins to quicken markedly. Her progression from passive sleepiness to active anger is first of all built into the growing periods defined by the groupings made by the alliterations and assonances of the poetry: she sings first two separate but parallel groups that follow the arch-like pattern a–b–b–a, c–d–d–c (e.g., *Tat–entzündet–zürnet–Tat* of the second group), then joins two of these groups together to form a larger arch of the form a–b–c–d–b–a–d–c (*Rechte–wahrt–Eide–hütet–wehret–Recht–herrscht–Meineid*). That this formal design in the poetry is perfectly followed by the musical design in both orchestral accompaniment and vocal line is a matter that the reader can discover for himself at leisure. Of particular interest here is the fashion in which rhythmic values, intervallic vocabulary, and tessitura of the vocal line express the increasing anger and intensity of Erda's speech. Her rhythmic values, especially on accented syllables, move from dotted crochet to semibreve; starting from G# near the bottom of her range she sweeps

Donald McIntyre as the Wanderer and Elizabeth Bainbridge as Erda at Covent Garden in Götz Friedrich's production designed by Josef Svoboda (photo: Reg Wilson)

gradually to an A♭ at its very top; starting from a relatively calm intervallic vocabulary of thirds and fourths, she moves through sixths, to sevenths, to octaves, finally climaxing in an astonishing diminished twelfth.

To notice the intricate poetic structure of a bit of text such as this, which is quite apart from its sense and deeply enmeshed in the musical structure, is to realize that the translator has, in addition to the usual problems of conveying the sense and capturing the various kinds of diction in translation, problems of trying to preserve the poetic structure and its correspondence with the musical one.

The Wanderer-Erda scene, so clear and original in its musico-dramatic design, stands at the beginning of an act that is similarly clear and original. At its flanks are the two long and crucial dialogues between the Wanderer and Erda, and between Siegfried and Brünnhilde — the old guard and the new. In the centre is a lighter intermezzo, filled with a spirit of good-natured, almost fatherly banter on Wotan's part and youthful energy (and insensitivity) on Siegfried's. Wagner gave added seriousness to the scene when he revised it between 1851 and 1853, by inserting Wotan's wonderfully human eruption of temper, both a flash of anger at Siegfried's callow brashness and a last unwillingness to renounce what he has realized that he must renounce. This flash of anger serves musically as a means of building up to the violent moment of Siegfried's breaking of Wotan's spear with his sword, and dramatically as a foil to Wotan's sudden calm renunciation, giving his final departure immense weight coloured by personal tragedy.[6]

Complementing the Wanderer-Erda dialogue on the other side of this intermezzo is the meeting and dialogue between Siegfried and Brünnhilde, a scene as strong and simple in overall design as it is rich in detail. It begins with a sizable introduction, whose musical stops and starts and sudden changes of direction express formally Siegfried's newly experienced confusion and fearful hesitation. (They also result in the closest approximation of recitative style to be found in the late acts of *The Ring*.) There follows the awakening of Brünnhilde and the dialogue itself, again cast both musically and dramatically in a large arch form that is articulated by thematic-motivic material newly presented in this scene. At each side of the arch stand two love-duets — the first time two distinct characters (as opposed to the Rhinemaidens, who are three versions of the same character) have sung together in *The Ring*. In both duets the principal motifs introduced in the first duet, motifs [58] and [59], are built into powerful, song-like phrases. In the first duet the two sing of their love for each other, but neither is understanding correctly what the other means by 'love'. The centre of the arch is made up of a dialogue, where the dramatic situation becomes less stable as the two engage each other more closely in argument, leading to the restabilization of a changed dramatic situation in the duet at the end of the scene. The character whose will is predominant in shaping the changed situation at the end of this particular scene is Siegfried, and his insistence is expressed musically in the dialogue-centre of the scene by means of motif [56], the motif to which Wotan had prophesied Siegfried's inheritance of his power. (The extensive presence of this motif here also serves to knit together musically the opening and closing scenes of the Act.) The orchestra introduces motif [56] quietly at the end of Brünnhilde's very first speech after their initial duet. Soon however, she slows down and backs away, realizing that what Siegfried wants from her will mean the abandonment of her godhead. She is first puzzled, then begins actively to resist Siegfried's insistence. This central portion of her dialogue is articulated by the motif of Example 7, a fine example of a new motif produced by abstracting certain elements from previous motifs and transforming them by combining them with new elements. This motif combines the triplet triads of the Valkyries' galloping motif [34] with the accented opening turn of motif [36a], Wotan's motif of dejection, and transforms both by a wrenching, dissonant harmony and the plangent tones of the cor anglais. In reaction to this resistance, Siegfried shapes his answers around motif [56] and tries to push it through to a cadence (something that will happen only with the last phrase of the act).

[7]

A unique feature of the particular musico-dramatic arch that Wagner has designed here is that it is, so to speak, upside down. It begins at a peak of excitement, even exaltation, and it returns there for its end. The dramatic pacing slows down continually toward the centre, in reflection of Brünnhilde's hesitation and resistance. At the centre Wagner places a kind of antipode to the exalted excitement of the beginning and end. (In stage action, the antithesis of beginning and centre is expressed by Brünnhilde's covering her eyes in the centre of the scene, and then rejecting the light when Siegfried uncovers them to awaken her a second time.) To form this antipode, Wagner sets a sizable monologue by Brünnhilde near the centre of the scene to music based on the same material as the independent orchestral piece known as the *Siegfried Idyll*. As befits its separateness at the eye of the storm here, this thematic-motivic material stands almost entirely outside not only this scene but *The Ring* as a whole.[7] (One of the motifs, the first and principal one, never recurs; the second only twice, in incidental commentary.) In any case, the peaceful material at the beginning of the monologue represents Brünnhilde's last determined attempt at resistance. She is soon won over by Siegfried's urgent pushing forward of the tempo, his insistence on motif [56], and his increasingly frequent returns to the motivic material of their opening duet. Finally, with a shriek of laughter, she releases herself to be herself in love, and they join for the final duet.

As mentioned above, this duet returns to and puts into new combinations the material of the opening duet ([58] and [59]), completing the arch of the scene. With these it mixes motif [56], which had been the musical vehicle of Siegfried's insistence across the central dialogue. To this rich motivic mix it adds a new ingredient:

[8]

Birgit Nilsson as Brünnhilde at Covent Garden in 1962 (photo: Anthony Crickmay)

This final thematic unit of the act appropriately brings us full circle, for it is the last element in the motivic characterization of Siegfried's evolution from a simple youth with no focus for his considerable energies to a mature man. The athletic, leaping fourths of motif [47] from the beginning of Act One, after passing through the more controlled but still explosive intermediate stage of the forging song (Example 4 above), emerge finally as the triumphantly solid, diatonic four-measure phrase in C major of Example

Ann Howard as Erda at ENO (photo: John Garner)

8 (which also turns up as the central section of the *Siegfried Idyll*). The existence of motivic families such as this one, in Wagner's subconscious at least, seems demonstrated by a passage from a letter to Mathilde Wesendonck, written on July 9 1859, while Wagner was prodding his imagination for an appropriate bit of cheerful piping, by which the Shepherd might announce the approach of Isolde's ship in the third act of *Tristan*. Instead Example 8 came to the surface. With surprise, Wagner realized that he had heard from Siegfried. Typical immodest exuberance (and self-pitying posturing) led him to anticipate the brilliant conclusion this would make for his interrupted project. In fact, of course, he had to file away this tune in his memory for nearly ten years before he could place it in its proper context, thus rounding off and tying together the large shape of the whole opera and completing what would be the most difficult and protracted delivery among all his operatic children.

> Just think! As I was working on the happy shepherd's piping at the arrival of Isolde's ship the other day, there suddenly occurs to me a turn of melody that is still more jubilant, almost heroically jubilant, and yet remains quite folk-like. I was about to reject the whole thing when I finally realized that this tune does not belong to Tristan's shepherd, but was Siegfried incarnate. I immediately looked up the closing lines of Siegfried with Brünnhilde and recognized that my melody belongs to the words 'Sie ist mir ewig, / ist mir immer, / Erb' und Eigen, / Ein' und All', (She's mine forever, / she is my joy, / my wealth, my world, / my one and all!) — and so on. That will have an unbelievably bold and jubilant effect. So I was at a stroke back in *Siegfried*. Should I then not continue to believe in my life, in my — holding out?[8]

Radnor Urfung as Mime at Covent Garden (photo: Donald Southern)

Notes

[1] See Ernest Newman, *The Life of Richard Wagner*, 4 vols., vol. 2 (New York, 1955), p. 513
[2] *The Wagner Operas* (published in England as *Wagner Nights*) (New York and London, 1949).
[3] The leitmotif charts are restricted by their very format to motifs, and thus fail to register the importance of phrase and section.
[4] One should recall that the Wanderer himself had been involved in the loss of control here, as he had not been in the Wanderer-Mime scene. Here he ends the process of disintegration not by resolving it, but by stopping it dead with a single gesture of *force majeure*, which Wagner directs be followed by a long silence, as the deeply shaken Wanderer pulls himself together. The English National Opera recording, with Reginald Goodall and Norman Bailey, is one of the very few to give this silence its proper weight.
[5] *Cosima Wagner's Diaries*, ed. Martin Gregor-Dellin and Dietrich Mack, trans. Geoffrey Skelton, vol. 1 (New York, 1977), p. 73.
[6] The moment of the Wanderer's acceptance of the realization that he must renounce power, at the climax of the previous scene, is recalled at this point by a motivic recall of the music — motifs 24 and 25 — which had occurred immediately following the Wanderer's 'long silence' there. The abrupt and unusual tonal shift after the breaking of the spear, from A minor-major to the tragic key of C minor, recalls the similar shift at the climax of Wotan's monologue to Brünnhildde in Act Two, Scene Two of *The Valkyrie*, when he had articulated the idea of voluntary renunciation of power ('nur eines will ich noch; / das Ende, / das Ende!'). This density of musical reference adds further to the weight of the moment.
[7] Ernest Newman, *The Life of Richard Wagner*, vol. 3 (New York, 1956), pp. 271-75 and John Deathridge, 'Cataloguing Wagner', *The Musical Times* cxxiv (1983), pp. 95-96. Wagner's (and Ernest Newman's) claim that this material was initially conceived separately from *The Ring*, as a string quartet movement, during the early days of Wagner's romance with Cosima, then Hans von Bülow's wife, has recently been challenged by John Deathridge.[7]
[8] *Richard Wagner an Mathilde Wesendonck* (Berlin, 1908), p. 161. Translation by the author.

Set Svanholm as Siegfried, a role he sang at Bayreuth in 1942 and in which he made his debuts at the Met. in 1946 and at Covent Garden in 1948. (*Royal Opera House Archives*)

'Siegfried' in the Context of Wagner's Operatic Writing

Derrick Puffett

Siegfried, as is well known, has an extraordinarily complex history. The story has been told many times, most recently in a fascinating book by Patrick McCreless,[1] but it always bears retelling. Originally *Young Siegfried*, (*Der junge Siegfried*), the work was conceived as a prelude to *Siegfried's Death* (*Siegfrieds Tod*, Wagner's initial title for *Twilight of the Gods* or *Götterdämmerung*); later, of course, the composer decided to add two further 'preludes', *The Rhinegold* and *The Valkyrie*, thus creating the tetralogy as we know it. The libretto for *Young Siegfried* was written in 1851; the first musical sketches date from the same year. The next five years saw the composition and orchestration of *Rhinegold* and *Valkyrie*. It is necessary to be so precise about the different stages of work, for now things start to get complicated.

Wagner's composition methods varied from work to work; in the case of *Siegfried*, he used a different method for each act. Act One was written in two drafts, produced simultaneously: a 'preliminary draft' (to adopt the nomeclature used by the *New Grove*), which occupied Wagner from September 1856 to the middle of January 1857, and a 'developed draft', completed three weeks later. Concurrently with all this labour he had also been working on the orchestration, a task he finished on March 31. So much for the first act. Wagner must have found this method too exhausting, for in the case of the later acts he did not attempt to score as he went along. In May and June 1857 he drafted Act Two, Scene One and the beginning of Scene Two. But he was getting bored with *The Ring*, which had now absorbed him, without hope of performance, for nine years; and besides, his mind was becoming increasingly obsessed with ideas for *Tristan and Isolde*. On June 28 he told Liszt he had broken off work: 'I have led my young Siegfried to a beautiful forest solitude; there I have left him under a linden tree, and taken leave of him with heartfelt tears. He will be better off there than anywhere else.' But only two weeks later — perhaps because he feared losing the thread — he was back at work, finishing the act in draft on August 9. Now came the real break. The next twelve years saw the composition of *Tristan* (1857-9), the Paris revision of *Tannhäuser* (1860-1) and the composition of *The Mastersingers* (1862-7), as well as the production of all three; but Wagner did no further work on *Siegfried* other than orchestrating the second act in 1864-5. Act Three was not composed until 1869 (the year of the *Siegfried Idyll*) and fully orchestrated until 1871. The work was premiered in 1876, along with *Twilight of the Gods*, as part of the first Bayreuth Festival.

The reasons for Wagner's abandoning *Siegfried* in mid-composition, and only taking it up again twelve years later, are many and complex. What concerns us here are the artistic results of the delay. With its fifteen-year composition period, a period which saw the creation of two other full-length operas (as well as the revision of a third), *Siegfried* enjoys a uniquely rich relationship with Wagner's other works. This relationship exists on at least three levels, creating a variety of contexts in which the work may be seen. This is not just a matter of academic interest: anyone's enjoyment of a work can be enhanced by a knowledge of the various backgrounds against which it was written. And even a brief discussion may shed some light.

[1] *Wagner's 'Siegfried': Its Drama, History and Music* (Ann Arbor, 1982).

The most immediate 'context' for Siegfried — and the one most relevant to anyone coming to the work for the first time — is of course *The Ring*. If the cycle as a whole is a tragedy (comparisons with Greek drama have become almost obligatory in Wagner studies), *Siegfried* is a comedy-within-the-tragedy, providing the perfect foil to the darker events surrounding it. *Siegfried* is sometimes described as the scherzo of *The Ring*, though this description holds good only for the first two acts, with their atmosphere of enchantment and fairy tale. With Act Three we are back in the world of *Rhinegold* and *Valkyrie*.

The relation to the earlier operas of the cycle — and to *Twilight of the Gods* — is of course crucial. It can be discussed in terms of plot, characters and music. From the point of view of plot, *Siegfried* is crucial in introducing

Wolfgang Windgassen as Siegfried at Covent Garden in 1962 (photo: Houston Rogers, Theatre Museum)

the hero from which the opera takes its name; the hero of the cycle, in Wagner's initial conception of the work, before the emphasis passed to Wotan. The adventures of 'Young Siegfried' give the opera its particular dramatic shape. *Siegfried* is also crucial in effecting the one move of the ring, as an object, between *The Rhinegold* and *Twilight of the Gods* — from Fafner, who is therefore of pivotal importance in *Siegfied*'s action, to Siegfried himself (on whose finger it stays till he gives it to Brünnhilde in the prologue of *Twilight of the Gods*). The rest of the hoard stops in the dragon's cave throughout *Siegfried*; Siegfried collects the Tarnhelm, so important in *The Rhinegold* and *Twilight of the Gods*, but does not use it. The character of Siegfried, however, is only one element of the plot. On a deeper level the opera is crucial in that it presents the all-important scene (Act Three, Scene One) in which Wotan finally renounces his ambitions: Siegfried, ring, dragon, even

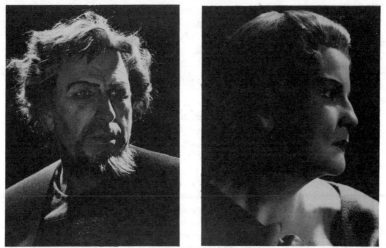

*Hans Hotter as the Wanderer and Astrid Varnay as Brünnhilde at Covent Garden in 1948
(photos: Houston Rogers, Theatre Museum; Donald Southern)*

the 'happy ending', all are ultimately irrelevant in the face of this
renunciation. We do not see Wotan again, though he remains a powerful
offstage presence.

Wotan is not the only character of whom we see the last. Mime is packed
off in Act Two, with a quick jab of Siegfried's sword; as is Fafner, after a
rather more strenuous struggle. Erda appears, for her one ghostly meeting
with Wotan, and then vanishes — presumably for ever. Alberich is not
altogether finished with yet: he makes two relatively brief appearances
in Act Two (apart from an offstage laugh when his brother is put to
death) and then withdraws, only to reappear in *Twilight of the Gods*.
Act Two of *Siegfried* sees his only meeting, after *Rhinegold*, with Wotan —
'black Alberich' and 'light Alberich' brought together again at last. Wotan

*Constance Shacklock as Erda and Otakar Kraus as Alberich at Covent Garden in 1954
(photo: Derek Allen)*

45

himself is transformed for the duration of *Siegfried* into the Wanderer, a magnificent but ultimately tragic figure who proves no match for the young hero. Act Three is important not only for Wotan's renunciation but for bringing his daughter, Brünnhilde, together with his grandson; their relationship is to become the main target of Alberich's plotting.

Musically, *Siegfried* serves to introduce a whole new batch of themes into *The Ring*. Those associated with Siegfried himself have a vigorous, animated quality which contrasts vividly with the brooding atmosphere of the previous dramas in the cycle; it even affects the music of other characters, notably Mime. Other important new themes in *Siegfried* are the chords associated with the Wanderer, first heard on his entrance in Act One; the 'Forest Murmurs' heard repeatedly in Act Two; the 'World Deliverance' motif, with which Wotan finally, in Act Three [56], accepts his fate, and the music incorporated into the *Siegfried Idyll*. *Siegfried* is not only important for these new themes: it also begins a long process of musical recapitulation. The first act prelude (composed some time before the rest of the opera, perhaps even before the rest of the cycle) revives the Nibelheim music from *Rhinegold*, along with its characteristic tonality; the next music we hear is that associated with the dragon. Both have been absent from *The Valkyrie*, apart from the occasional passing reference. The Siegfried material is new, but Mime's conversation with the Wanderer is a large-scale recapitulation of earlier themes. In Act Two, the prelude ('Fafner's Repose', as Wagner liked to call it) brings references to Alberich, curse, gold and ring — all largely absent from *The Valkyrie* — as first Alberich, then Wotan and finally Fafner himself appear. The 'Forest Murmurs' that dominate the second half of the act are repeatedly interrupted, by Fafner, Mime and Alberich, all of whom retire from the work in their different ways before the curtain falls. Wotan's dialogue with Erda in Act Three involves much recapitulation, but by now there is more restatement than statement, as in Siegfried's brush with the Wanderer, a scene which entails rehearing in condensed form all the material associated with the hero's early life. The rest of the work combines new and old material in ever-changing ways, most curiously in the use of the *Idyll* music — new in the context of *The Ring*, familiar from that of Wagner's domestic life. For a few minutes *Siegfried* takes on yet another dimension, one which can seem almost surrealistic in the opera house.

*

The 'context' provided by *The Ring* is a necessary structural framework, a precondition without which *Siegfried*, the individual opera, would not exist. But there is another context, one which forces itself on the attention no less pressingly even though it is a mere by-product of the circumstances of composition. Between the drafting of Acts Two and Three there elapsed a period of twelve years, during which Wagner wrote *Tristan* and *The Mastersingers*; it is impossible to listen to *Siegfried* Act Three without being reminded of the fact. The interdependence of all three works is obvious from the sketches. Robert Bailey, who has described them in detail, writes of Wagner's restless mood during the major part of 1857, 'a period of constant shifting between work on *Siegfried* and a growing interest in *Tristan*'.[2] Bailey quotes a sketch actually marked 'Third act [i.e. of *Siegfried*] or

[2] 'The Method of Composition', *The Wagner Companion*, ed. Peter Burbidge and Richard Sutton (London, 1979), p. 315.

Alberto Remedios as Siegfried and Rita Hunter as Brünnhilde in the production by Glen Byam Shaw and John Blatchley at ENO (photo: John Garner)

Act Three of Wolfgang Wagner's Bayreuth production, 1974 (photo: Festspielleitung Bayreuth)

Tristan'; we recognise it as the music heard in *Siegfried* Act Three at the mention of Grane, Brünnhilde's horse. Another sketch, dating from May 1857, was originally intended for Siegfried's words '*Sang'st du mir nicht, dein Wissen sei das Leuchten der Liebe zu mir?*' ('You said that all your wisdom came by the light of your love for me.'), only to be set aside and used for *Tristan*. (Siegfried's words were completely reharmonised, to a version of the World Inheritance motif [56].) Between *Siegfried* and *The Mastersingers* there is less overlap: while working on *The Mastersingers* Act Two Wagner sketched a phrase which looks a little like the Act Three chorale but eventually became the World Inheritance motif, but this example is exceptional. And only one *Siegfried* theme — the 'bold and jubilant' horn melody referred to at the end of Anthony Newcomb's essay — was conceived during the composition of *Tristan*.

The musical relationship, however, is clear; so clear that when listening to *Siegfried* Act Three we sometimes wonder if we are not listening to *Tristan* (less frequently, *The Mastersingers*) instead. The effect is oddly disorientating, much more so than when similar things happen in *Twilight of the Gods*. It is almost as if we have been hearing two different operas, two different *Siegfried*s, composed 'before and after *Tristan*'. After the pastoral fun and games of Acts One and Two we are plunged back into the world of myth; and the musical expression of that world is the familiar stock of leitmotifs, incomparably intensified through their contact with Wagner's new harmonic language. (Indeed it seems that one of the reasons why he postponed completion of the work in 1857 was that he wanted the later parts of *The Ring* to be more chromatic; for this he needed the experience of writing *Tristan*.) The diatonic, 'closed' song forms such as we find in the first two acts — Wagner here approaches closer than at any other time to Singspiel — give way to the chromatic, developmental writing typical of the later *Ring*. It is largely a matter of density, of the rate at which things happen. Given the new freedom of harmony, musical events can succeed each other at a speed never possible before, creating bold juxtapositions and undreamt-of possibilities of leitmotivic reference. Imagine Siegfried's meeting with the Wanderer in the 'old' style: the cumbersome lengths, the one-dimensional textures, the early-Wagnerian limitation (which so infuriated Nietzsche) of only being able to say one thing at a time. Here the contrasts are abrupt, the textures constantly changing, the whole treatment of the text much more fluid and responsive. All this has become possible through the composition of *Tristan*.

One must go on from this, however, and admit the essential unity of *Siegfried*; for whatever our feelings of disorientation when hearing the last act, the opera is clearly, audibly and demonstrably one work. This is partly because all three acts use the same leitmotifs, as Anthony Newcomb has pointed out, but it is also a matter of tonal structure. The leitmotifs and other recurring formal elements create between them a network of tonal and harmonic relationships which unify the work as surely as any purely thematic connections. They also serve to forge links with the other operas in the cycle: thus not only does the B flat minor of the first act prelude recall the Nibelheim scene from *Rhinegold*, but the C major of the final curtain looks forward to the C minor of the Funeral March in *Twilight of the Gods*. These tonal links operate at a deeper level of the structure than any similarities or differences of style.

At the same time, the sheer accomplishment of Wagner's new manner, the incredible advance in technique, creates problems he could not possibly have anticipated. As Joseph Kerman has written, 'Between 1857 and 1869 . . . his style had of course matured very significantly; but he was stuck with his old leitmotifs. One must indeed admire the skill with which he managed to transform some of them to suit his astonishingly sleek new developmental style — that "art of transition", as he called it, which in *Twilight of the Gods* sometimes sounds like ripe Richard Strauss. But the discrepancy between the musical process and the crudeness of some of the themes — the Ride of the Valkyries theme, for example, goes all the way back to those 1850 sketches — has always been glaringly obvious.'[3] This is too harsh: 'crudeness' in Wagner is nearly always part of a dramatic intention (one would hardly want the Valkyries to appear *refined*). But many writers have been troubled, in *Siegfried* Act Three, by what can only be described as Wagner's uncertainty: uncertainty of style, uncertainty of tone, uncertainty of whatever it was that led him, after the wonders and audacities of the Wotan-Erda scene, to end his opera with a C major duet in which the voices actually sing together. Robert Gutman, one of Wagner's biographers, sees the Wotan-Erda scene as the composer's 'emotional, sad farewell' to the ideal of the 'complete art work'; music drama was now to give way to grand opera — the genre in which *Twilight of the Gods* was originally conceived.[4]

Again, this is too harsh. The stylistic 'uncertainties' in *Siegfried*, like the stylistic dichotomy between the second and third acts, were largely a result of the protracted timetable to which the work was composed (a period of fifteen years, from 1856 to 1871, and even that excludes the 1851 sketches). Of

[3] 'Wagner and Wagnerism', *The New York Review of Books* (December 22, 1983), p. 30.
[4] *Richard Wagner: The Man, His Mind and His Music* (Harmondsworth, 1971), p. 423.

all Wagner's operas *Siegfried* was spread over much the longest time. The result — if we look at it positively rather than negatively — is a *Tannhäuser*-like division of styles, a division which has its own dramatic expressiveness. Siegfried comes of age when he meets Wotan, and so does the music; the grandson's rejection of his grandfather, the only means by which he can proceed to 'the heights', is counterpointed in Wagner's own outgrowing of his earlier musical idiom. On a deeper level, the return to the world of myth in Act Three requires a more complex means of expression, one which Wagner simply did not have at his disposal in 1857. Who can doubt that he did right to wait? In any case, the stylistic differences apparent within *Siegfried* flatten out considerably when the work is taken in the context of the cycle as a whole. The leitmotifs used in *Siegfried* are making a much longer journey; similarly, Wagner's musical styles in *The Ring* — which he likes to manipulate, as coolly as any Stravinsky, for dramatic effect — are like the landscapes of his texts, always subtly changing yet always recognisably part of the same universe.

*

This brings us to the last context in which *Siegfried* must be seen: the context provided by Wagner's other operatic works. (One could go on to include his non-operatic works, the operatic works of other composers, the entire history of music: there is no end to it.) Perhaps the most intriguing comparison is with *Parsifal*: the 'pure fool' who must learn pity, just as Siegfried must learn fear. Both characters undergo a spiritual or psychological progress, as well as the more obvious physical one; and this provides the story of the opera. Here too we may find parallels with Tannhäuser, Tristan and even Walther von Stolzing. Then there are parallels between *pairs* of characters. Siegfried's relationship with Mime seems to anticipate Tristan's with Melot, itself an inversion of the Tristan-Kurwenal pairing in the same opera; and Siegfried's relationship with the Wanderer prefigures Tristan's with King Marke, and even Walther's with Hans Sachs. These are deep waters, too deep to enter here. On a purely musical level, we have seen how simple contrasts of style, which were so important in *Tannhäuser* and *Tristan*, and will become the predominant mode of organisation in *Parsifal*, are in *Siegfried* given a new intensity whose effects are felt throughout the entire *Ring* cycle. Such contrasts are in fact a conventional means of musical characterisation, not only in Wagner but throughout the entire operatic repertory.

*

The danger involved in all these comparisons is of losing sight of *Siegfried*'s particularity, of what makes it unique among Wagner's output. Again, a brief discussion must suffice. On the level of subject, *Siegfried* was of course the work in which Wagner projected most clearly his ideal of the 'New German' hero, the 'man of the future' who can exist only through the destruction of the present. *Siegfried* too is the opera that links Wagner most closely with Nietzsche, who on his first visit to the composer heard him trying out the chords to which Brünnhilde sings the words '*Verwundet hat mich, der mich erweckt*' ('He who has awakened me has wounded me' — as Ernest Newman remarked, it was an omen). Nietzsche's Zarathustra shares many of Siegfried's traits. From Nietzsche through *Zarathustra* to Richard Strauss: the sheer energy of *Siegfried* must surely have influenced the later composer, who was once observed weeping during the third act.

Derek Hammond-Stroud as Alberich and Gwynne Howell as the Wanderer in the ENO production designed by Ralph Koltai in 1978 (photo: John Garner)

The musical structure of the work has several unusual features. Its first act comes perilously close to number opera (hence the feeling of *Singspiel*); while the rapidity of changing scenes and textures in Act Two, like some of the orchestration, has a kaleidoscopic effect not too far removed from Mahler, whose performance of the work in London was reviewed by Shaw. *Siegfried* is the only Wagner opera that ends with a duet, unless we count *Tristan* (whose *Liebestod* recapitulates part of the love duet from the second act) — but the C major 'glare', conveying more brightness than warmth, is closer to *The Mastersingers*. The duet ending perhaps suggests the temporary nature of Siegfried's achievement: as McCreless points out, we have only to wait until the first, ominous chords of *Twilight of the Gods* for that achievement to be put in perspective.

Within *The Ring*, however — as within Wagner's output as a whole — *Siegfried* is a climax of exuberance and vitality, its 'scherzo' character rivalled only by *The Mastersingers*. 'We all breathed that vast orchestral atmosphere of fire, air, earth, and water, with unbounded relief and invigoration ...': Shaw's reaction is typical, and has been echoed since by countless audiences.

Acts One and Two of Patrice Chéreau's 1980 production, designed by Richard Peduzzi, at Bayreuth with Heinz Zednik as Mime, Manfred Jung as Siegfried and Fritz Hübner as Fafner (photos: Festspielleitung Bayreuth)

Acts One and Two of 'Siegfried' in the 1983 Bayreuth 'Ring' produced by Peter Hall with designs by William Dudley. Siegmund Nimsgern as the Wanderer, Peter Haage as Mime and Manfred Jung as Siegfried (photos: Festspielleitung Bayreuth)

Thematic Guide

Each Opera Guide to a part of *The Ring* refers to one general list of leitmotifs in which the themes are numbered according to their first appearance in the cycle. Only the principal ones that occur in *Siegfried* are given here.

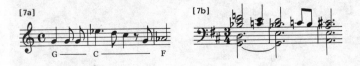

[8]

[9a]

[9b]

[10]

[11]

[12]

[13a]

[13b]

[14]

[15]

[16a] [16b]

[17]

[18]

[19] or

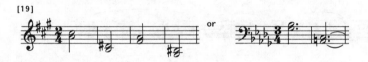

[20]

[21]

[22]

[23]

[24]

[25]

[26]

[27]

[28]

[29]

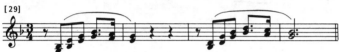

[30]

[31]

[32]

[33]

[34]

[35]

[36a]

[36b]

[37]

[38]

[39]

[40]

[41]

58

[42]

[43]

[44]

[45]　　　　　　　[46] i.e. [27] + [45]

[47]

[48a]

[48b]

[49a]

[49b]

[49c]

[50]

[51]

OR

[52]

[53a]

[53b]

[53c] i.e. [2]

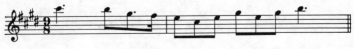

[53d]

[54] i.e. [27] + [53c]

[55]

11b, 30a

[56]

[57] i.e. [21]

[58]

[59]

[60]

[61]

[67]

61

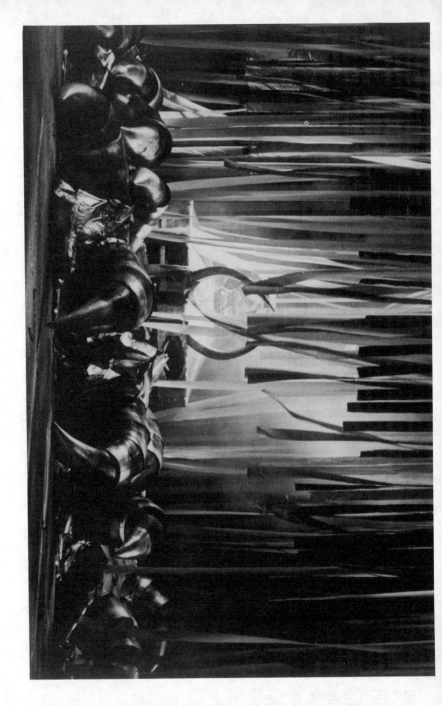

Fafner the dragon in Act Two of the production by Götz Friedrich at Covent Garden, designed by Josef Svoboda with costumes by Ingrid Rosell (photo: Reg Wilson)

Siegfried

Second day of the Festival Play
'The Ring of the Nibelung'

Music-Drama in Three Acts by Richard Wagner

Poem by Richard Wagner

English translation by Andrew Porter

Siegfried was first performed at the Festspielhaus, Bayreuth on August 16, 1876. The first performance in England was at Her Majesty's Theatre, London on May 7, 1882. The first performance in the United States was at the Metropolitan Opera House, New York on November 9, 1887.

This translation was commissioned by English National Opera (then Sadler's Wells Opera) and first performed at the London Coliseum in January 29, 1970. The full cycle was first given in July and August, 1973 and the opera was recorded in full performance at the London Coliseum in December 1975 by EMI.

The German text for the whole cycle was first published in 1853. Archaisms of spelling and an excess of punctuation have been removed but the original verse layout has been retained.

The stage directions are literal translations of those written by Wagner and do not reflect any actual production. The numbers in square brackets refer to the Thematic Guide.

CHARACTERS

Siegfried	*tenor*
Mime	*tenor*
The Wanderer	*bass*
Alberich	*bass*
Fafner	*bass*
Erda	*contralto*
Brünnhilde	*soprano*
Voice of the Woodbird	*soprano*

Act One

A forest. The forestage represents part of a cave in the rocks, extending inwards more deeply to the left, but occupying about three-quarters of the stage-depth to the right. There are two natural entrances to the forest, the one to the right opening directly, and the other, broader one opening sideways, to the background. Against the rear wall, to the left, is a big forge, formed naturally in the rocks; only the large bellows are artificial. A rough natural chimney passes through the roof of the cave. A very large anvil and other smith's tools. [19, 20, 17, 5x, 6, 27]

Scene One. *Mime is sitting at the anvil and with increasing anxiety hammers at a sword; at length he stops working disconsolately.*

MIME

Wearisome labour!		Zwangvolle Plage!
Work till I drop!		Müh' ohne Zweck!
The strongest sword	[17, 5x]	Das beste Schwert,
I struggle to make,		das je ich geschweisst,
an amazing weapon,		in der Riesen Fäusten
fit for a giant:		hielte es fest!
but when I have made it,		doch dem ich's geschmiedet,
that insolent Siegfried		der schmähliche Knabe,
just laughs and snaps it in two,		er knickt und schmeisst es entzwei,
as though I'd made him a toy!		als schüf ich Kindergeschmeid'!

(Mime crossly throws the sword on the anvil, slumps on to his arms, [19] *and gazes at the ground in thought.)*

I know one sword	[27a]	Es gibt ein Schwert,
that could not be shattered:		das er nicht zerschwänge:
Notung's fragments		Notungs Trümmer
he never would break,		zertrotzt' er mir nicht,
if only I could forge,		Könnt' ich die starken
those pieces,	[5x]	Stücken schweissen,
if but my skill		die meine Kunst
could achieve that deed!		nicht zu kitten weiss!
If I could forge those fragments,	[9a]	Könnt ich's dem Kühnen schmieden,
all my shame would change into joy!		meiner Schmach erlangt' ich da Lohn!

(He leans back further and lowers his head in thought.) [19, 21]

Fafner, the mighty dragon,		Fafner, der wilde Wurm,
lies there within those woods		lagert im finstren Wald;
and protects with his monstrous bulk		mit des furchtbaren Leibes Wucht
the Nibelung gold,		der Niblungen Hort
guarding it well.	[21]	hütert er dort.
Siegfried's conquering strength		Siegfrieds kindischer Kraft
could quickly lay Fafner low:		erläge wohl Fafners Leib:
the Nibelung's ring	[6]	des Niblungen Ring
would then come to me.		erränge er mir.
And one sword is all that I need,	[27]	Nur ein Schwert taugt zu der Tat;
and Notung only will serve,		nur Notung nützt meinem Neid,
when Siegfried deals him the blow:	[27, 8b, 13a]	wenn Siegfried sehrend ihn schwingt:
and I cannot forge it,		und ich kann's nicht schweissen,
Notung, the sword!	[17]	Notung, das Schwert!

(He has readjusted the sword, and returns to his hammering in deepest dejection.)

Wearisome labour!	Zwangvolle Plage!
Work till I drop!	Müh' ohne Zweck!
The strongest sword	Das beste Schwert,
that ever I make	das je ich geschweisst,
will prove too weak	nie taugt es je
for that one mighty deed!	zu der einzigen Tat!
I tinker and tap away	Ich tappre und hämmre nur,
because Siegfried commands:	weil der Knabe es heischt:
he laughs and snaps it in two,	er knickt und schmeisst es entzwei
and scolds me, if I don't work!	und schmäht doch, schmied ich ihm nicht!

(He drops the hammer.)

SIEGFRIED

(*In rough forest clothes, with a silver horn slung from a chain, he bursts in exuberantly from the forest. He has tethered a large bear with a rope, and in boisterous high spirits he sets it on Mime.*) [45]

Hoiho! Hoiho!	Hoiho! Hoiho!
Come on! Come in!	Hau ein! Hau ein!
Bite him! Bite him,	Friss ihn! Friss ihn,
the lazy smith!	den Fratzenschmied!

(*He laughs. Mime drops the sword in fright, and runs behind the forge. Siegfried urges the bear to chase him about.*)

MIME

Off with that beast!	Fort mit dem Tier!
Why bring me a bear?	Was taugt mir der Bär?

SIEGRIED

He came with me	Zu zwei komm ich,
to teach you to hurry!	dich besser zu zwicken:
Bruin, beg for the sword!	Brauner, frag nach dem Schwert!

MIME

Hey! let him go!	He! Lass das Wild!
There lies your weapon,	Dort liegt die Waffe:
forged and finished today.	fertig fegt' ich sie heut.

SIEGFRIED

Well, then today you are free!	So fährst du heute noch heil!

(*He unties the bear, and gives him a flick on the rump with the rope.*)

Off, Bruin!	Lauf, Brauner,
You're needed no more.	dich brauch ich nicht mehr!

(*The bear lopes back into the forest.*)

MIME
(*comes out trembling from behind the hearth.*)

To killing bears	Wohl leid ich's gern,
I've no objection,	erlegst du Bären:
but why bring live ones	Was bringst du lebend
inside the cave?	die Braunen heim?

SIEGFRIED
(*sits down to recover from his laughter.*)

I wanted a better comrade	Nach bessrem Gesellen sucht' ich,
than the one I leave at home;	als daheim mir einer sitzt;
and so I called with my horn,	im tiefen Walde mein Horn
set the forest glades resounding:	liess ich hallend da ertönen:
Would I find what I longed for,	ob sich froh mir gesellte
a faithful friend? —	ein guter Freund,
that's what I asked with my call!	[45] das frug ich mit dem Getön!
From the bushes came a bear,	Aus dem Busche kam ein Bär,
who growled as I played my tune;	der hörte mir brummend zu;
and I liked him better than you —	er gefiel mir besser als du,
though better still I shall find!	doch bessre fänd' ich wohl noch!
So I bridled him	Mit dem zähen Baste
and brought him along	zäumt' ich ihn da,
to see if the sword had been finished.	dich, Schelm, nach dem Schwerte zu fragen.

(*He jumps up and goes across to the anvil.*)

MIME
(*takes the sword to give to Siegfried.*)

I made it keen and sharp,	Ich schuf die Waffe scharf,
and its shine will gladden your heart.	ihrer Schneide wirst du dich freun.

(*Anxiously he holds on to it, but Siegfried wrenches it violently from him.*)

SIEGFRIED

What use is the shiny sharpness	Was frommt seine helle Schneide,
if the steel's not hard and true!	ist der Stahl nicht hart und fest!

(testing the sword with his hand) [39]

Hey! what a useless	Hei! Was ist das
thing you have made!	für müss'ger Tand!
A feeble pin!	Den schwachen Stift
Call it a sword?	nennst du ein Schwert?

(He smashes it on the anvil, so that the splinters fly about. Mime shrinks in terror.) [47]

Well, there are the pieces,	Da hast du die Stücken,
blundering boaster;	schändlicher Stümper:
I should have smashed it	hätt' ich am Schädel
there on your brainpan!	dir sie zerschlagen!
Now will the liar	Soll mich der Prahler
brag any longer,	Länger noch prellen?
talking of giants, [12]	Schwatzt mir von Riesen
and boldness in battle,	und rüstigen Kämpfen,
and deeds of daring,	von Kühnen Taten
and fearless defence?	und tüchtiger Wehr;
And weapons you'll forge me,	will Waffen mir schmieden,
swords you'll fashion,	Schwerte schaffen;
praising your skill,	rühmt seine Kunst,
and proud of your craft?	als könnt' er was Rechts:
Yet when I handle	nehm' ich zur Hand nun,
what you have fashioned —	was er gehämmert,
a single blow	mit einem Griff
destroys all your trash!	zergreif ich den Quark!
If he were not	Wär' mir nicht schier
too mean for my rage,	zu schäbig der Wicht,
I should fling in the fire	ich zerschmiedet' ihn selbst
the smith and his works —	mit seinem Geschmeid,
the aged doddering dwarf!	den alten albernen Alp!
My anger would then have an end!	Des Ärgers dann hätt' ich ein End'!

(In a rage Siegfried flings himself down on a stone seat to the right. Mime cautiously keeps out of his way.) [47]

MIME

Again you rage like a fool,	Nun tobst du wieder wie toll:
ungrateful, heartless boy!	dein Undank, traun, ist arg!
Maybe today I've failed you;	Mach ich dem bösen Buben
but when my work is not good	nicht alles gleich zu best,
then you at once forget [17]	wach ich ihm Gutes schuf,
the good things I have done!	vergisst er gar zu schnell!
Must I once more remind you	Willst du denn nie gedenken,
that you should be more grateful?	was ich dich lehr' vom Danke?
And you should learn to obey me,	Dem sollst du willig gehorchen,
who always showed you such love.	der je sich wohl dir erwies.

(Siegfried turns away crossly, his face to the wall, his back to Mime.) [45]

Now once again you're not listening!	Das willst du wieder nicht hören

(He stands perplexed, and then goes to the cooking pots at the fireplace.)

But food is what you need:	Doch speisen magst du wohl?
come, try this meat I have roasted;	Vom Spiesse bring ich den Braten:
or would you prefer this soup?	versuchtest du gern den Sud?
For you, all is prepared.	Für dich sott ich ihn gar.

(He brings food to Siegfried, who without turning round knocks bowl and meat out of Mime's hands.)

SIEGFRIED

Meat I roast for myself:	Braten briet ich mir selbst:
you can drink your slops alone!	deinen Sudel sauf allein!

MIME
(in a querulous screech)

Fine reward	Das ist nun der Liebe
for all my loving care!	schlimmer Lohn!
Thus the boy repays	Das der Sorgen
what I've done!	schmählicher Sold!
A whimpering babe, [17]	Als zullendes Kind
born in these woods —	zog ich dich auf,

Mime was kind	wärmte mit Kleiden
of the tiny mite;	den kleinen Wurm:
feeding you well,	Speise und Trank
keeping you warm,	trug ich dir zu,
sheltering you safe	hütete dich
as my very self.	wie die eigne Haut.
And when you grew older	Und wie du erwuchsest,
I was your nurse;	wartet' ich dein;
when you were sleepy	dein Lager schuf ich,
I smoothed your bed.	dass leicht du schliefst.
I made you nice toys	Dir schmiedet' ich Tand
and that shining horn, [45]	und ein tönend Horn;
toiling away,	dich zu erfreun,
trying to please:	müht' ich mich froh.
my clever counsels	Mit klugem Rate
sharpened your wits;	riet ich dir klug,
I tried to make you	mit lichtem Wissen
crafty and bright.	lehrt' ich dich Witz.
Staying at home	Sitz' ich daheim
I slave and sweat,	in Fleiss und Schweiss,
while you go	nach Herzenslust
wandering around.	schweifst du umher.
I toil for your pleasure,	Für dich nur in Plage,
think only of you,	in Pein nur für dich
I wear myself out —	verzehr ich mich alter,
a poor old dwarf!	armer Zwerg!

(sobbing)

Then you repay me [5x]	Und aller Lasten
for all that I've done	ist das nun mein Lohn,
with your furious scolding	dass der hastige Knabe
and scorn and hate!	mich quält und hasst!

(Siegfried has turned round again and looks steadily into Mime's eyes. Mime encounters his gaze and tries timidly to conceal his own.)

SIEGFRIED
[47]

Much you've taught to me, Mime,	Vieles lehrtest du, Mime,
and many things I have learnt;	und manches lernt' ich von dir;
but one thing you most long to teach me,	doch was du am liebsten mich lehrtest,
that lesson I never learn:	zu lernen gelang mir nie:
how not to loathe your sight.	wie ich dich leiden könnt'.
When you bring food [47, 17]	Trägst du mir Trank
and offer me drink,	und Speise herbei,
my hunger turns to disgust;	der Ekel speist mich allein;
when you prepare	schaffst du ein leichtes
soft beds for my rest,	Lager zum Schlaf,
then sleep is driven away;	der Schlummer wird mir da schwer;
when you would make me	willst du mich weisen,
clever and wise,	witzig zu sein,
I would be deaf and dull.	gern bleib ich taub und dumm.
I am repelled	Seh ich dir erst
by the sight of you;	mit den Augen zu,
I see that you're evil	zu übel erkenn ich,
in all that you do.	was alles du tust:
I watch you stand,	Seh ich dich stehn,
shuffle and nod,	gangeln und gehn,
shrinking and slinking,	knicken und nicken,
with your eyelids blinking —	mit den Augen zwicken:
by your nodding neck	beim Genick möcht' ich
I'd like to catch you,	den Nicker packen,
and end your shrinking,	den Garaus geben
and stop your blinking!	dem garst'gen Zwicker!
So deeply, Mime, I loathe you.	So lernt' ich, Mime, dich leiden.
If you're so clever,	Bist du nun weise,
then tell me something	so hilf mir wissen,
which long I have sought in vain:	worüber umsonst ich sann:

through the woods roaming,
trying to avoid you —
what is it makes me return?
  Everything to me
  is dearer than you:
  birds in branches
  and fish in the brook —
  all are dear to me,
  far more than you.
What is it then makes me return?
If you're wise, then tell me that.

MIME
(sits facing him, familiarly, but at a little distance.) [48a]

My child, that shows quite clearly
how dear to your heart I must be.

SIEGFRIED
(laughing)

I cannot bear the sight of you —
have you forgotten that?

MIME
(shrinks back, and sits down again at the side, facing Siegfried.)

That comes from your wild young heart, [17]
from a wildness you must tame.
Young ones are ever yearning [48a]
after their parents' nest;
love is the cause of that yearning:
and that's why you yearn for me:
you love your dear old Mime —
  you must learn to love me!
What the mother-birds are to fledglings,
while in the nest they lie,
long before they can flutter,
such to you, dearest child,
is wise and careful old Mime —
  such must Mime be!

SIEGFRIED

Hey, Mime, if you're so clever,
there's something else you can teach me!
  The birds were singing [48a]
  so sweetly in spring; [30]
their songs were loving and tender:
  and you replied,
  when I asked you why,
that they were mothers and fathers.
  They chattered so fondly, [48b]
  and never apart;
  then building a nest,
  they brooded inside;
  and soon little fledglings
  were fluttering there; [47]
the parents cared for the brood.
  And here in the woods [48a, 30]
  the deer lay in pairs,
and savage foxes and wolves, too:
  food was brought to the den
  by the father, [48a]
the mother suckled the young ones.
  I learnt from them [48b]
  what love must be;
  I never disturbed them
  or stole their cubs.
You must tell me, Mime,

in den Wald lauf ich,
dich zu verlassen,
wie kommt das, kehr ich zurück?
  Alle Tiere sind
  mir teurer als du:
  Baum und Vogel,
  die Fische im Bach,
  lieber mag ich sie
  leiden als dich:
Wie kommt das nun, kehr ich zurück?
Bist du klug, so tu mir's kund.

Mein Kind, das lehrt dich kennen,
wie lieb ich am Herzen dir lieg.

Ich kann dich ja nicht leiden,
vergiss das nicht so leicht!

Des ist deine Wildheit schuld,
die du, Böser, bänd'gen sollst.
Jammernd verlangen Junge
nach ihrer Alten Nest;
Liebe ist das Verlangen:
So lechzest du auch nach mir,
so liebst du auch deinen Mime —
  so musst du ihn lieben!
Was dem Vögelein ist der Vogel,
wenn er im Nest es nährt,
eh' das flügge mag fliegen:
das ist dir kind'schem Spross
der kundig sorgende Mime —
  das muss er dir sein!

Ei, Mime, bist du so witzig,
so lass mich eines noch wissen!
  Es sangen die Vöglein
  so selig im Lenz,
das eine lockte das andre:
  Du sagtest selbst,
  da ich's wissen wollt',
das wären Männchen und Weibchen.
  Sie kosten so lieblich
  und liessen sich nicht;
  sie bauten ein Nest
  und brüteten drin;
  da flatterte junges
  Geflügel auf,
und beide pflegten der Brut.
  So ruhten im Busch
  auch Rehe gepaart,
selbst wilde Füchse and Wölfe:
  Nahrung brachte
  zum Nest das Männchen,
das Weibchen säugte die Welpen.
  Da lernt' ich wohl,
  Was Liebe sei:
  der Mutter entwand ich
  die Welpen nie.
Wo hast du nun, Mime,

where your dear little wife is.
Where is my mother, tell me!

dein minniges Weibchen,
dass ich es Mutter nenne?

MIME
(*crossly*)

Why do you ask?
Don't be so dull!
For you're not a bird or a fox!

Was ist dir, Tor?
Ach, bist du dumm!
Bist doch weder Vogel noch Fuchs?

SIEGFRIED

'A whimpering babe,
born in these woods,
Mime was kind
to the tiny mite . . . '
But who created
that whimpering babe?
For making a babe
needs a mother too!

'Das zullende Kind
zogest du auf,
wärmtest mit Kleiden
den kleinen Wurm':
Wie kam dir aber
der kindische Wurm?
Du machtest wohl gar
ohne Mutter mich?

MIME
(*in great embarrassment*)

I'll explain it;
try to believe me:
I am your father
and mother in one.

Glauben sollst du,
was ich dir sage:
ich bin dir Vater
und Mutter zugleich.

SIEGFRIED

You're lying, foul little dwarf!
Every young one is like his parents;
I know, for I've seen it myself.
One day in the shining stream
    I could see every tree
    and forest creature,
    sun and shadow,
    just as they are,
reflected below in the brook.
    And there in the stream
    I saw my face —
    it wasn't like yours,
    not in the least,
    no more than a toad
    resembles a fish.
No fish had a toad for a father!

[47] Das lügst du, garstiger Gauch!
Wie die Jungen den Alten gleichen,
das hab ich mir glücklich ersehn.
Nun kam ich zum klaren Bach:
    da erspäht' ich die Bäum'
[53a] und Tier' im Spiegel;
    Sonn' und Wolken,
    wie sie nur sind,
[39] im Glitzer erschienen sie gleich.
    Sa sah ich denn auch
[33] mein eigen Bild;
    ganz anders als du
    dünkt' ich mir da:
[17, 5] so glich wohl der Kröte
[1b] ein glänzender Fisch;
doch kroch nie ein Fisch aus der Kröte!

MIME
(*very crossly*)

What an absurd
and stupid idea!

Greulichen Unsinn
kramst du da aus!

SIEGFRIED
(*with increasing animation*)

See here, at last
    it's clear to me,
what before I pondered in vain:
    through the woods I wandered
    trying to avoid you —
do you know why I returned?

[47, 48a] Siehst du, nun fällt
    auch selbst mir ein,
was zuvor umsonst ich besann:
    wenn zum Wald ich laufe,
    dich zu verlassen,
wie das kommt, kehr ich doch heim?

(*He leaps up.*)

Because you alone can inform me
what father and mother are mine!

Von dir erst muss ich erfahren,
wer Vater und Mutter mir sei!

MIME
(*shrinking from him*)

What father? What mother?
Meaningless question!

Was Vater! Was Mutter!
Müssige Frage!

SIEGFRIED
(seizes him by the throat.)

Well then I must choke you,	[47]	So muss ich dich fassen,
force you to tell me!		um was zu wissen:
All kindness		gutwillig
is wasted on you!		erfahr ich doch nichts!
You'll only answer		So musst' ich alles
when I strike you.		ab dir trotzen:
If I had not forced you		kaum das Reden
to teach me,		hätt' ich erraten,
I would not even know		entwand ich's mit Gewalt
how to speak!		nicht dem Schuft!
Now out with it,		Heraus damit,
rascally wretch!		räudiger Kerl!
Who are my father and mother?		Wer ist mir Vater und Mutter?

MIME
(having nodded his head and made signs with his hands, is released by Siegfried.)

You nearly choked me to death!		Ans Leben gehst du mir schier!
Let go! What you're eager to learn		Nun lass! Was zu wissen dich geizt,
I'll tell you, all that I know.		erfahr es, ganz wie ich's weiss.
O hard-hearted	[17]	O undankbares,
ungrateful child!		arges Kind!
Now hear, and learn why you hate me!		Jetzt hör, wofür du mich hassest!
I'm not your father,		Nicht bin ich Vater
nor kin to you,		noch Vetter dir,
and yet you owe everything to me!		und dennoch verdankst du mir dich!
You're no kin to me,		Ganz fremd bist du mir,
and yet I was kind,		dem einzigen Freund;
and my pity alone		aus Erbarmen allein
gave you this home:		barg ich dich hier:
a fine reward I receive!		nun hab ich lieblichen Lohn!
What a stupid fool I have been!	[31, 29]	Was verhofft' ich Tor mir auch Dank?
I found once in the wood		Einst lag wimmernd ein Weib
a woman who lay and wept:		da draussen im wilden Wald:
I helped her here to my cave,		zur Höhle half ich ihr her,
and by the fire there I warmed her.	[30]	am warmen Herd sie zu hüten.
A child stirred in her body;		Ein Kind trug sie im Schosse;
sadly she gave it birth.		traurig gebar sie's hier;
That birth was cruel and hard;		sie wand sich hin und her,
I helped as best I could.		ich half, so gut ich konnt'.
Great was her pain! She died.		Gross war die Not! Sie starb,
But Siegfried, you were born.	[39]	doch Siegfried, der genas.

SIEGFRIED
(lost in thought) [31]

She died, my mother, through me?	So starb meine Mutter an mir?

MIME

To my charge she entrusted the child:		Meinem Schutz übergab sie dich:
I gladly cared for you.		ich schenkt' ihn gern dem Kind.
What love I lavished on you!		Was hat sich Mime gemüht,
What kindness and care you received!		was gab sich der Gute für Not!
'A whimpering babe,	[17]	'Als zullendes Kind
born in these woods . . .'		zog ich dich auf . . .'

SIEGFRIED

I think I have heard that before!	[31]	Mich dünkt, des gedachtest du schon!
But say: why am I called Siegfried?	[39]	Jetzt sag: woher heiss ich Siegfried?

MIME

The wish of your mother —	So, hiess mich die Mutter,
that's what she told me:	möcht' ich dich heissen:
as 'Siegfried' you would grow	als 'Siegfried' würdest
strong and fair.	du stark und schön.

'And Mime was kind
to the tiny mite...'

[17] 'Ich wärmte mit Kleiden
den kleinen Wurm...'

SIEGFRIED

Now tell me the name of my mother.

[31] Nun melde, wie hiess meine Mutter?

MIME

Her name I hardly knew.
  'Feeding you well,
  keeping you warm...'

Das weiss ich wahrlich kaum!
[17]   'Speise und Trank
  trug ich dir zu...'

SIEGFRIED

Her name I told you to tell me!

[31] Den Namen sollst du mir nennen!

MIME

Her name I forget. No, wait!
Sieglinde, now I remember;
I'm sure that that was her name.
  'And sheltering you safe
  as my very self...'

Entfiel er mir wohl? Doch halt!
Sieglinde mochte sie heissen,
die dich in Sorge mir gab.
[17]   'Ich hütete dich
  wie die eigne Haut...'

SIEGFRIED
(*ever more urgently*)

Now tell me, who was my father?

[31] Dann frag ich, wie hiess mein Vater?

MIME
(*roughly*)

His name I never knew!

Den hab ich nie gesehn.

SIEGFRIED

Did my mother say what his name was?

Doch die Mutter nannte den Namen?

MIME

He fell in battle —
that's all that she said.
the tiny orphan
was left in my care;
  'And as you grew older
  I was your nurse;
  when you were sleepy
  I smoothed your bed...'

Erschlagen sei er,
das sagte sie nur;
dich Vaterlosen
befahl sie mir da.
[17]   'Und wie du erwuchsest,
  wartet' ich dein;
  dein Lager schuf ich,
  dass leicht du schliefst...'

SIEGFRIED

Stop that eternal
snivelling!
If I am to trust your story,
if truth at last you're speaking,
then I must see some proof!

Still mit dem alten
[48] Starenlied!
Soll ich der Kunde glauben,
hast du mir nichts gelogen,
so lass mich Zeichen sehn!

MIME

But what proof can I show you?

Was soll dir's noch bezeugen?

SIEGFRIED

I trust you not with my ears;
my eyes alone I'll believe:
what witness can you show?

Dir glaub ich nicht mit dem Ohr,
dir glaub ich nur mit dem Aug':
Welch Zeichen zeugt für dich?

MIME
(*reflects for a moment* [19] *and then fetches the two pieces of a broken sword.*) [27, 17]

This, this your mother gave me
for payment, food, and service,
this was my wretched wage.
Look here, just a broken sword!
She said your father had borne it
when he fought his last, and was killed.

Das gab mir deine Mutter:
[5x] für Mühe, Kost und Pflege
Liess sie's als schwachen Lohn.
Sieh her, ein zerbrochnes Schwert!
Dein Vater, sagte sie, führt' es,
als im letzten Kampf er erlag.

And now these fragments
Mime will forge me:
I've found my father's sword!
So! Hurry up, Mime!
Back to your work;
show me your skill;
employ all your craft!
Cheat me no more
with worthless trash.
These fragments alone
serve for my sword!
But if I find
flaws in your work,
if you should spoil it,
this splendid steel,
you'll feel my blows on your hide;
I'll make you shine like the steel!
Today, I swear, hear me!
I will have my sword;
the weapon today shall be mine.

Und diese Stücken
[47] dann schwing ich mein rechtes Schwert!
Auf! Eile dich, Mime!
Mühe dich rasch;
kannst du was Rechts,
nun zeig deine Kunst!
Täusche mich nicht
mit schlechtem Tand:
[27] den Trümmern allein
trau ich was zu!
Find ich dich faul,
fügst du sie schlecht,
flickst du mit Flausen
den festen Stahl,
dir Feigem fahr ich zu Leib,
das Fegen lernst du von mir!
Denn heute noch, schwör ich,
will ich das Schwert;
die Waffe gewinn ich noch heut!

MIME
(*alarmed*)

But why do you need it today?

Was willst du noch heut mit dem Schwert?

SIEGFRIED

Through the wide world
I shall wander,
never more to return!
I am free now,
I can leave you,
nothing binds me to you!
My father you are not,
in the world I'll find my home!
Your hearth is not my house,
I can leave your rocky lair.
As the fish swims
through the waters,
as the bird flies
through the branches,
so I shall fly,
floating afar,
like the wind through the wood
wafting away!
Then, Mime, I'll never return.

Aus dem Wald fort
in die Welt ziehn:
nimmer kehr ich zürück!
Wie ich froh bin,
dass ich frei ward,
nichts mich bindet und zwingt!
[47] Mein Vater bist du nicht;
in der Ferne bin ich heim;
dein Herd ist nicht mein Haus,
meine Decke nicht dein Dach.
Wie der Fisch froh
in der Flut schwimmt,
wie der Fink frei
sich davonschwingt:
[67] flieg ich von hier,
flute davon,
wie der Wind übern Wald
weh ich dahin,
dich, Mime, nie wieder zu sehn!

(*He rushes out into the forest.*)

MIME
(*in utmost anxiety*)

Siegfried! Hear me!
Hear me! Come back!

Halte! Halte!
Halte! Wohin?

(*He calls into the forest at the top of his voice.*)

Hey! Siegfried!
Siegfried! Hey!

He! Siegfried!
Siegfried! He!

(*He gazes in astonishment as Siegfried rushes away, then returns to the forge and sits behind the anvil.*)

He storms away!
And I sit here,
my former cares
joined by a new one.
I'm helpless, caught in my trap!
Now what can I say?
And when he returns
then how can I lead him

[5] Da stürmt er hin!
[6] Nun sitz ich da:
zur alten Not
hab ich die neue;
[17] vernagelt bin ich nun ganz!
[19] Wie helf ich mir jetzt?
Wie halt ich ihn fest?
[21] Wie führ ich den Huien

to Fafner's lair? | zu Fafners Nest?
I can't forge these pieces [5x] | Wie füg ich die Stücken
of obstinate steel! | des tückischen Stahls?
For no fire of mine | Keines Ofens Glut
can ever fuse them; | glüht mir die echten:
nor can Mime's hammer | keines Zwergen Hammer
conquer their hardness. | zwingt mir die harten.
This Nibelung hate, [7b] | Des Niblungen Neid,
toil and sweat, | Not und Schweiss
cannot make Notung new, [49a]nietet mir Notung nicht,
can't forge the sword once again! | schweisst mir das Schwert nicht zu ganz!

(Mime slumps in despair on the stool behind the anvil.)

Scene Two. *The Wanderer (Wotan) comes in from the forest by the entrance at the back of the cave. He is wearing a long dark-blue cloak, and uses his spear as a staff. On his head is a large hat with a broad, round brim, which hangs down over his missing eye.*

WANDERER

Hail there, worthy smith! | Heil dir, weiser Schmied!
This wayweary guest [49b]Dem wegmüden Gast
asks to rest | gönne hold
awhile by your fire! | des Hauses Herd!

MIME
(starting up in fright) [20]

Who's there? Who has sought me | Wer ist's, der im wilden
here in the woods? | Walde mich sucht?
Who disturbs me in my retreat? | Wer verfolgt mich im öden Forst?

WANDERER
(very slowly, advancing just a step at a time)

'Wanderer', so I am called: [49a]'Wand'rer' heisst mich die Welt;
widely I have roamed | weit wandert' ich schon:
on the earth's broad surface [49b] auf der Erde Rücken
travelling afar. | rührt' ich mich viel.

MIME

Then travel some more [17] | So rühre dich fort
live up to your name; | und raste nicht hier,
let the Wanderer move on! | nennt dich 'Wand'rer' die Welt!

WANDERER

Good men ever give me welcome; [49c]Gastlich ruht' ich bei Guten,
gifts from many have I gained; | Gaben gönnten viele mir:
for ill fate falls only | denn Unheil fürchtet,
on evil men. | wer unhold ist.

MIME

Ill fate haunts me | Unheil wohnte
here in my home; | immer bei mir:
why do you seek to increase it? | willst du dem Armen es mehren?

WANDERER
(still advancing slowly)

Much I sought for, [49b] | Viel erforsch' ich,
and much I found, | erkannte viel:
I have often | Wicht'ges konnt' ich
taught men wisdom, | manchem künden,
often lightened | manchem wehren,
heavy sorrows, | was ihr mühte,
eased their afflicted hearts. | nagende Herzensnot.

MIME

Much you have learnt, [20] | Spürtest du klug
maybe much you have found; | und erspähtest du viel,
but don't you come seeking in my house. | hier brauch ich nicht Spürer noch Späher.

I don't need you,
and I live alone.
Loiterers cannot stay here.

[49a] Einsam will ich
und einzeln sein,
Lungerern lass' ich den Lauf.

WANDERER
(*again advancing a little*)

Many fancy
wisdom is theirs,
but what they most need,
that they don't know.
When they ask me,
freely I answer:
wisdom flows from my words.

[49c] Mancher wähnte
weise zu sein,
nur was ihm not tat,
wusste er nicht;
[49b] was ihm frommte,
liess er erfragen:
lohnend lehrt' ihr mein Wort.

MIME
(*increasingly uneasy, as he watches the Wanderer approach*)

Useless knowledge
many ask for,
but I know all that I need.

Müss'ges Wissen
wahren manche:
[17] ich weiss mir grade genug.

(*The Wanderer has advanced right up to the hearth.*)

And my wits are good;
I want no more.
So, wise one, be on your way!

Mir genügt mein Witz,
ich will nicht mehr:
dir Weisem weis ich den Weg!

WANDERER
(*sitting at the hearth*) [9a]

I sit by your hearth,
and wager my head —
it's yours if I prove not wise.
My head is yours,
it falls to your hand,
if I, when you ask
all you want,
fail to redeem it aright.

Hier sitz ich am Herd
[49a] und setze mein Haupt
der Wissenswette zum Pfand:
Mein Kopf ist dein,
du hast ihn erkiest,
entfrägst du mir nicht,
was dir frommt,
lös ich's mit Lehren nicht ein.

MIME
(*has been staring open-mouthed at the Wanderer; he shudders, and says timorously to himself:*) [17]

How can I get rid of this spy?
I'll ask him three tricky questions.

[19] Wie werd' ich den Lauernden los?
Verfänglich muss ich ihn fragen.

(*He recovers himself with an effort.*)

Your head pays me
if you fail:
take care, use cunning to save it!
Three the questions
that I shall ask!

[9a] Dein Haupt pfänd ich
für den Herd:
nun sorg, es sinnig zu lösen!
Drei der Fragen
stell ich mir frei.

WANDERER

Three times I must answer.

Dreimal muss ich's treffen.
[17, 9a, 19]

MIME
(*He racks his brains.*)

You've wandered so far
on the earth's surface,
and long you've roamed through the world:
and so you should know
what dusky race
dwells in the earth's deep caverns?

[49b] Du rührtest dich viel
auf der Erde Rücken,
[8a, 17] die Welt durchwandertst du weit:
[19] Nun sage mir schlau:
welches Geschlecht
tagt in der Erde Tiefe?

WANDERER

In the earth's deep caverns —
that's where the Niblungs dwell;
Nibelheim is their land.
Black elves, those Niblungs;

In der Erde Tiefe
[17] tagen die Nibelungen:
Nibelheim ist ihr Land.
Schwarzalben sind sie;

Black-Alberich	Schwarz-Alberich
once was their master and lord!	[6] hütet' als Herrscher sie einst!
By a magic ring's	Eines Zauberringes
all-conquering spell,	zwingende Kraft
he ruled that hard-working race.	[5x] zähmt' ihm das fleissige Volk.
Richest treasures,	[20] Reicher Schätze
shimmering gold,	schimmernden Hort
he made them find,	[8b] häuften sie ihm:
to buy all the world for his kingdom — [17, 9a]	der sollte die Welt ihm gewinnen.
I've answered: what else would you ask?	Zum zweiten, was frägst du, Zwerg?

MIME
(thinking still harder) [17, 19]

Much, Wanderer,	[49b] Viel, Wanderer,
much you know	weisst du mir
of the earth's dark secret caves.	[8a, 17] aus der Erde Nabelnest:
But can now you say,	[19] Nun sage mir schlicht,
what mighty race	[12] welches Geschlecht
dwells on the earth's broad surface?	ruht auf der Erde Rücken?

WANDERER

On the earth's broad surface —	Auf der Erde Rücken
that's where the giants dwell;	[12] wuchtet der Riesen Geschlecht:
Riesenheim is their land.	Riesenheim ist ihr Land.
Fasolt and Fafner,	Fasolt und Fafner,
the giants' chieftains,	[12] der Rauhen Fürsten,
envied the Nibelung's might;	neideten Nibelungs Macht;
and his powerful hoard	[19] den gewaltigen Hort
they gained for themselves —	gewannen sie sich,
and in that hoard was the ring.	errangen mit ihm den Ring.
To gain that treasure	[6] Um den entbrannte
the brothers fought,	den Brüdern Streit;
and Fasolt fell then.	[5x, 21] der Fasolt fällte,
In dragon shape	als wilder Wurm
Fafner now guards all the gold. —	hütet nun Fafner den Hort. —
One question still you have left.	[9a] Die dritte Frage nun droht.

MIME
(rapt in thought) [17, 19]

Much, Wanderer,	[49b] Viel, Wanderer,
much you know	weisst du mir
of the earth and all her dwellers.	[8a, 17] von der Erde rauhem Rücken.
But can now you say	[19] Nun sage mir wahr,
what lordly race	welches Geschlecht
dwells on cloud-hidden heights?	wohnt auf wolkigen Höhn?

WANDERER

On cloud-hidden heights —	Auf wolkigen Höhn
that's where the gods dwell;	[8] wohnen die Götter:
Walhall is their home.	Walhall heisst ihr Saal.
Light-spirits are they;	Lichtalben sind sie;
Light-Alberich,	Licht-Alberich,
Wotan, rules over that clan.	Wotan, waltet der Schar.
From the world-ashtree's	[1b] Aus der Welt-Esche
sacred branches	weihlichstem Aste
Wotan once tore his spear:	[9a] schuf er sich einen Schaft:
dead the tree —	dorrt der Stamm,
but still mighty the spear;	nie verdirbt doch der Speer;
and with that spear-point	[60] mit seiner Spitze
Wotan rules the world.	sperrt Wotan die Welt.
Bargains and contracts,	Heil'ger Verträge
bonds and treaties,	Treuerunen
deep in that shaft he graved.	[5x] schnitt in den Schaft er ein.
Who holds that spear-shaft	Den Haft der Welt
rules the world;	hält in der Hand,
and that spear-shaft	wer den Speer führt,

by Wotan's hand is held.	[5x, 17] den Wotans Faust umspannt.
In thrall to him	Ihm neigte sich
the Nibelung band;	[6] der Niblungen Heer;
the giants' strong race	der Riesen Gezücht
bows to his will;	zähmte sein Rat:
all must obey him as master —	[49a]ewig gehorchen sie alle
the spear's all-powerful lord.	[9a] des Speeres starkem Herrn.

(after carefully observing the Wanderer with the spear, now falls into a state of great anxiety, searches for his tools in confusion, and timidly looks away.) [17]

The answers were right;	Fragen und Haupt
your head is safe:	[49a] hast du gelöst:
now, Wanderer, go on your way!	nun, Wand'rer, geh deines Wegs!

WANDERER

What you needed to know	[49b] Was zu wissen dir frommt,
you should have asked me,	solltest du fragen:
while I had wagered my head.	[49a, 9a] Kunde verbürgte mein Kopf.
You merely asked me	Dass du nun nicht weisst,
what you knew,	was dir frommt,
so now we'll stake your head in turn.	des fass ich jetzt deines als Pfand.
You refused greeting	[49c] Gastlich nicht
to your guest,	galt mir dein Gruss,
and so I had	mein Haupt gab ich
to risk my head	in deine Hand,
to gain some rest at your hearth.	un mich des Herdes zu freun.
The law demands	Nach Wettens Pflicht
your head in turn,	pfänd ich nun dich,
if you should fail	[9a] lösest du drei
to answer me well.	der Fragen nicht leicht.
So Nibelung, sharpen your wits!	Drum frische dir, Mime, den Mut!

MIME
(very timidly and hesitantly, eventually composing himself in nervous resignation) [17, 48]

I left home	Lang schon mied ich
many years ago;	mein Heimatland,
years ago I left	lang schon schied ich
my mother's womb.	aus der Mutter Schoss;
I shrink beneath Wotan's glances;	[8] mir leuchtete Wotans Auge,
he came to spy in my cave:	zur Höhle lugt' er herein;
his glance frightens	vor ihm magert
my wits away.	mein Mutterwitz.
But now I must try to be wise;	[50] Doch frommt mir's nun, weise zu sein,
Wanderer, ask what you will!	Wandrer, frage denn zu!
Perhaps good luck will help me;	[19] Vielleicht glückt mir's, gezwungen
the dwarf still can save his head?	zu lösen des Zwergen Haupt.

WANDERER
(again seating himself comfortably) [8a]

Now, worthiest dwarf,	Nun, ehrlicher Zwerg,
answer me truly:	[33] sag mir zum ersten:
What is the name of the race	welches ist das Geschlecht,
that Wotan treated harshly	dem Wotan schlimm sich zeigte
and yet holds most dear in his heart?	[44] und das doch das liebste ihm lebt?

MIME
(gaining courage) [17, 50]

I'm no expert	Wenig hört ich
in heroes' histories	von Heldensippen;
but what you ask is easy to guess.	der Frage doch mach ich mich frei.
The Wälsungs must be	[33] Die Wälsungen sind
that chosen race	das Wunschgeschlecht,
that Wotan cared for	das Wotan zeugte
and loved so dearly,	und zärtlich liebte,
though he was cruel and harsh:	zeigt' er auch Ungunst ihm.

Arthur Fear as the Wanderer at Covent Garden in 1935 (Royal Opera House Archives)

Siegmund and Sieglinde,
children of Wälse,
that wild and desperate
twin-born pair.   [39]
Siegfried, he was their child,
the Wälsungs' brave mighty son.
So this time, Wanderer,   [17, 50]
have I saved my head?

Siegmund und Sieglind
stammten von Wälse,
ein wild-verzweifeltes
Zwillingspaar:
Siegfried zeugten sie selbst,
den stärksten Wälsungenspross.
Behalt ich, Wand'rer,
zum ersten mein Haupt?

WANDERER
(*pleasantly*)

Yes, it is safe,
for your answer was right:
it's not easy to catch you!   [13a]
But though you guessed   [8a]
the first one right,
my second may prove too hard.
A wily Niblung   [17, 19]
cared for Siegfried,
planned that he should kill Fafner,   [21]
gain the ring for the Niblung,
and make him lord of the world.
Name the sword
that Siegfried must strike with,
if he's to kill the foe.

Wie doch genau
das Geschlecht du mir nennst:
schlau eracht ich dich Argen!
Der ersten Frage
wardst du frei.
Zum zweiten nun sag mir, Zwerg:
ein weiser Niblung
wahret Siegfried;
Fafnern soll er ihm fällen,
dass den Ring er erränge,
des Hortes Herrscher zu sein.
Welches Schwert
muss Siegfried nun schwingen,
taug'es zu Fafners Tod?

MIME
(*forgetting more and more his present situation, and keenly interested in the topic, rubs his hands with pleasure.*) [17]

Notung, that's the name   [50]
of the sword,   [27]
the sword that Wotan struck
into an ashtree:
and one alone could win it,
he who could draw it forth.
Where mighty warriors
struggled in vain,
Siegfried the Wälsung
drew it forth;
thus he mastered the sword,
till by Wotan's spear it was snapped.
Now the bits are saved
by a wily smith;
for he knows that only
with Wotan's sword
a brave but foolish boy,   [39]
Siegfried, can kill the dragon.   [27]
(highly delighted) [50]
Now twice the dwarf
has rescued his head?

Notung heisst
ein neidliches Schwert;
in einer Esche Stamm
stiess es Wotan:
dem sollt' es geziemen,
der aus dem Stamm es zög'.
Der stärksten Helden
keiner bestand's:
Siegmund, der Kühne,
konnt's allein:
fechtend führt' er's im Streit,
bis an Wotans Speer es zersprang.
Nun verwahrt die Stücken
ein weiser Schmied;
denn er weiss, dass allein
mit dem Wotansschwert
ein kühnes dummes Kind,
Siegfried, den Wurm versehrt.
Behalt ich Zwerg
auch zweitens mein Haupt?

WANDERER
(*laughing*) [17, 50]

The wittiest
and the wiliest Niblung!
the cleverest dwarf I've known!
But since you're so wise
to use for your purpose
the youthful strength of the hero,
let me ask
the final question now.
Tell me, you wily
weapon-smith: [17]
Whose hand can make new those
fragments?
Notung, the sword — who will forge it?   [39]

Der witzigste bist du
unter den Weisen:
wer kam' dir an Klugheit gleich?
Doch bist du so klug,
den kindischen Helden
für Zwergenzwecke zu nützen,
mit der dritten Frage
droh ich nun!
Sag mir, du weiser
Waffenschmied:
wer wird aus den starken Stücken
Notung, das Schwert, wohl schweissen?

(jumps up in extreme terror.) [47]

The fragments! The sword!		Die Stücken! Das Schwert!
Alas! You've caught me!		O weh! Mir schwindelt!
What can I say?		Was fang ich an?
What can I do?		Was fällt mir ein?
Accursed steel!		Verfluchter Stahl,
Would I'd never seen it!		dass ich dich gestohlen!
To me it has brought		Er hat mich vernagelt
only pain and woe!	[5x]	in Pein und Not!
Stubborn and hard,		Mir bleibt er hart,
my hand cannot weld it;		ich kann ihn nicht hämmern;
heat and hammer,		Niet' und Löte
all are in vain!		lässt mich im Stich!

(As if demented, he throws his tools about, and gives way to complete despair.)

The wisest of smiths	[17]	Der weiseste Schmied
fails at the task.		weiss sich nicht Rat!
Who can forge that sword	[7b]	Wer schweisst nun das Schwert,
if my hand fails?		schaff ich es nicht?
How can I give you an answer?		Das Wunder, wie soll ich's wissen?

(has risen calmly from the hearth.) [49a]

Thrice you asked me your questions,		Dreimal solltest du fragen,
thrice I answered you right:		dreimal stand ich dir frei:
but what you asked		nach eitlen Fernen
was meaningless;		forschtest du;
you gave no thought to your need,	[7b]	doch was zunächst dir sich fand,
failed to ask what you required.		was dir nützt, fiel dir nicht ein.
Now when I tell it	[27]	Nun ich's errate,
you'll feel despair.	[9a, 17]	wirst du verrückt:
Your wily head		gewonnen hab ich
I can claim as my prize!		das witzige Haupt!
So, Fafner's dauntless destroyer,		Jetzt, Fafners kühner Bezwinger,
hear, you wretched dwarf:	[21]	hör, verfallner Zwerg:
'One who has never		'Nur wer das Fürchten
learnt to fear —	[27]	nie erfuhr,
he makes Notung new.'		schmiedet Notung neu.'

(Mime stares at him wide-eyed; he turns to go.) [13b]

Your wily head —		Dein weises Haupt
guard it with care!		wahre von heut:
I leave it forfeit to him	[39]	verfallen lass ich es dem,
who has never learnt to fear.		der das Fürchten nicht gelernt!

(He turns away smiling and disappears quickly into the forest. As if crushed, Mime has sunk down on the stool behind the anvil.)

Scene Three. *Mime stares out before him into the sunlit forest, and begins to tremble violently.* [13b, 21]

Accursed light!	[14]	Verfluchtes Licht!
The air is aflame!	[13a]	Was flammt dort die Luft?
What's flickering and flashing,	[13b]	Was flackert und lackert,
what flutters and swirls,		was flimmert und schwirrt,
what floats in the air		was schwebt dort und webt
and swirls in the wind?		und wabert umher?
What glistens and gleams		Dort glimmert's und glitzt's
in the sun's bright glow?		in der Sonne Glut!
What hisses and hums		Was säuselt und summt
and roars so loud?		und saust nun gar?
It growls and heaves,		Es brummt und braust
comes crashing this way!		und prasselt hieher!
It breaks through the trees;		Dort bricht's durch den Wald,
where can I hide?		will auf mich zu!

(He leaps up in terror.)

The threatening monster	Ein grässlicher Rachen
opens its jaws;	reisst sich mir auf:
the dragon will catch me!	der Wurm will mich fangen!
Fafner! Fafner!	Fafner! Fafner!

(*With a shriek he collapses behind the anvil.*) [27]

(*breaks out of the bushes and calls out, still off-stage, his movements evident from the snapping of the undergrowth.*)

| Hey there! You idler! | Heda, du Fauler! |
| Say, have you finished? [67] | Bist du nun fertig? |

(*He enters the cave and pauses in surprise.*) [47]

Quick, I've come for my sword.	Schnell, wie steht's mit dem Schwert?
But where's the smith?	Wo steckt der Schmied?
Stolen away?	Stahl er sich fort?
Hey, hey! Mime, you coward!	Hehe, Mime, du Memme!
Where are you! Come out, I say!	Wo bist du? Wo birgst du dich?

MIME
(*in a feeble voice, from behind the anvil*) [21]

| It's you then, child? | Bist du es, Kind? |
| Are you alone? | Kommst du allein? |

SIEGFRIED
(*laughing*)

Under the anvil? [47]	Hinter dem Amboss?
Say, what work took you there?	Sag, was schufest du dort?
Were you sharpening my sword?	Schärftest du mir das Schwert?

MIME
(*coming out much confused and disturbed*)

| The sword? The sword? [21] | Das Schwert? Das Schwert? |
| How can I forge it? | Wie möcht' ich's schweissen? |

(*half to himself*)

'One who has never	'Nur wer das Fürchten
learnt to fear — [27]	nie erfuhr,
he makes Notung new.'	schmiedet Notung neu.'
So how could I	Zu weise ward ich
undertake such work?	für solches Werk!

SIEGFRIED
(*violently*)]47]

| Give me an answer! | Wirst du mir reden? |
| Want me to help you? | Soll ich dir raten? |

MIME
(*as before*)

No man can help in my need.	[13b]Wo nähm' ich redlichen Rat?
My wily head —	[49a] Mein weises Haupt
I had to stake it.	hab ich verwettet:
I've lost it; it's forfeit to him	[39] verfallen, verlor ich's an den,
'who has never learned to fear'.	[19] 'der das Fürchten nicht gelernt'.

SIEGFRIED
(*impatiently*)

| Trying to escape me? [47] | Sind mir das Flausen? |
| Still no reply? | Willst du mir fliehn? |

MIME
(*gradually recovering himself a little*)

I fear this youth	Wohl flöh' ich dem,
who knows not fear! [17]	der's Fürchten kennt!
But wait: though I was eager to teach him,	Doch das liess ich dem Kinde zu lehren!
yet, fool I forgot	Ich Dummer vergass,
to teach him fear.	was einzig gut,

Love was the main thing that I tried for; but alas, that lesson failed! So how can I teach him to fear?	[48a] Liebe zu mir sollt' er lernen; das gelang nun leider faul! [13b]Wie bring ich das Fürchten ihm bei?

SIEGFRIED
(seizes him.)

Well, must I help you? What work has been done?	[47] He! Muss ich helfen? Was fegtest du heut?

MIME

I thought of your good; I sank into brooding, thinking of weighty things to teach you.	Um dich nur besorgt, versank ich in Sinnen, wie ich dich Wichtiges wiese.

SIEGFRIED
(laughing)

You certainly sank — under the anvil: what weighty advice did you find?	Bis unter den Sitz warst du versunken: Was Wichtiges fandest du da?

MIME
(steadily regaining self-possession)

What fear is, that's what I learnt; that's what I mean to teach you.	Das Fürchten lernt' ich für dich, dass ich's dich Dummen lehre.

SIEGFRIED
(with quiet curiosity)

And what can this fear be?	Was ist's mit dem Fürchten?

MIME

You've not learnt to fear, and you'd leave the wood, go forth in the world? What use is the mightiest sword till you can fear as well?	Erfuhrst du's noch nie und willst aus dem Wald [27] doch fort in die Welt? Was frommte das festeste Schwert, blieb dir das Fürchten fern?

SIEGFRIED
(impatiently) [17]

Foolish words I hear from your lips!	Faulen Rat erfindest du wohl?

MIME
(approaching Siegfried ever more confidingly) [31, 17]

They are your mother's words, heard from her lips — words that I promised one day I'd teach you. In the wide wicked world I shan't let you venture, until you can fear as well.	Deiner Mutter Rat redet aus mir; was ich gelobte, muss ich nun lösen: in die listige Welt dich nicht zu entlassen, eh' du nicht das Fürchten gelernt.

SIEGFRIED
(brusquely) [47]

Is it a skill, a craft I should learn? Then speak, and teach me what fear is!	Ist's eine Kunst, was kenn ich sie nicht? Heraus! Was ist's mit dem Fürchten?

MIME

Have you not felt within the woods, as darkness fell, in dusky glades, a dreadful whisper — hum and hiss — savage, growling	[13b] Fühltest du nie im finst'ren Wald, bei Dämmerschein am dunklen Ort, wenn fern es säuselt, summst und saust, wildes Brummen

sounds draw near?
Dazzling flashes
wildly flicker;
howling, roaring
assail your ears.
Have you not felt mysterious horrors
that threaten to harm you?
shivering and shaking,
quivering and quaking,
while your heart trembles and faints,
wildly hammers and leaps?
Till you have felt these things,
then fear to you is unknown.

näher braust,
[14] wirres Flackern
um dich flimmert,
schwellend Schwirren
zu Leib dir schwebt:
fühltest du dann nicht grieselnd
Grausen die Glieder dir fahen?
[43] Glühender Schauer
schüttelt die Glieder,
in der Brust bebend und bang
berstet hämmernd das Herz?
Fühltest du das noch nicht,
das Fürchten blieb dir noch fremd.

SIEGFRIED
(*thoughtfully*) [43]

Wonderful feelings
those must be!
Yet my heart
firmly beats in my breast.
The shivering and shaking,
the glowing and sinking,
burning and fainting,
trembling and quaking —
I am yearning to feel them.
When may I taste these joys?
Can I learn them,
Mime, from you?
How can a coward instruct me?

Sonderlich seltsam
muss das sein!
[39] Hart und fest,
fühl ich, steht mir das Herz.
[14] Das Grieseln und Grausen,
das Glühen und Schauern,
Hitzen und Schwindeln,
Hämmern und Beben:
gern begehr ich das Bangen,
[43] sehnend verlangt mich's der Lust!
Doch wie bringst du,
Mime, mir's bei?
Wie wärst du, Memme, mir Meister?

MIME

Easily learnt!
The way I know well:
brooding brought it to mind.
I know where a dragon dwells,
who lives and feeds on men.
Fear you'll learn from Fafner;
follow me; we'll find his den.

[21] Folge mir nur,
ich führe dich wohl:
[43] sinnend fand ich es aus.
[21] Ich weiss einen schlimmen Wurm,
der wügt' und schlang schon viel:
Fafner lehrt dich das Fürchten,
folgst du mir zu seinem Nest.

SIEGFRIED

And where is his den?

[43] Wo liegt er im Nest?

MIME

Neidhöhle,
that's what it's called:
to the east, at the edge of the wood.

Neidhöhle
wird es genannt:
im Ost, am Ende des Walds.

SIEGFRIED

Is that not near to the world?

Dann wär's nicht weit von der Welt?

MIME

From Neidhöhl the world isn't far.

Bei Neidhöhle liegt sie ganz nah.

SIEGFRIED

Then lead me on to your Fafner.
Fear he can teach me,
then forth to the world!
Now quick! Forge me the sword!
In the world I have to wield it.

Dahin denn sollst du mich führen:
Lernt' ich das Fürchten,
dann fort in die Welt!
Drum schnell! Schaffe das Schwert,
in der Welt will ich es schwingen.

MIME

The sword? Ah no!

[47] Das Schwert? O Not!

SIEGFRIED

On with your forging!
Show me your skill!

Rasch in die Schmiede!
Weis, was du schufst!

Accursed steel!
My skill is too weak for the task.
No dwarf can forge it
or master the magic spell.
One who fear does not know —
he might more easily succeed.

[5x]
[17] Verfluchter Stahl!
Zu flicken versteh ich ihn nicht:
den zähen Zauber
bezwingt keines Zwergen Kraft.
Wer das Fürchten nicht kennt,
der fänd' wohl eher die Kunst.

SIEGFRIED

Lazy scoundrel,
lying to cheat me,
making excuses,
trying to delay.
So Mime is too weak for the task!
Give me the fragments;
I'll have to teach you!
(striding to the hearth)
My father's sword
yields to his son;
and I'll forge it myself!

Feine Finten
weiss mir der Faule;
dass er ein Stümper,
sollt' er gestehn:
nun lügt er sich listig heraus!
Her mit den Stücken,
[46] fort mit dem Stümper!
Des Vaters Stahl
fügt sich wohl mir:
[27] ich selbst schweisse das Schwert!

(He sets to work impetuously, throwing Mime's tools about.) [45]

MIME

If you'd been careful
to learn your craft,
then now you would have your reward;
but you were always
lazy and slow,
and now you'll wish you'd obeyed me.

Hättest du fleissig
die Kunst gepflegt,
[17] jetzt käm' dir's wahrlich zugut:
doch lässig warst du
stets in der Lehr':
was willst du Rechtes nun rüsten?

SIEGFRIED

When my teacher has failed,
could I be succesful
if I had always obeyed?
(He cocks a snook at him.)
So move aside,
out of my way,
or else with the sword I'll forge you!

Was der Meister nicht kann,
vermöcht' es der Knabe,
hätt' er ihm immer gehorcht?
Jetzt mach dich fort,
misch dich nicht drein:
sonst fällst du mir mit ins Feuer!

(He has heaped up a mass of charcoal on the hearth, and he keeps the fire going while he fixes the fragments of the sword in a vice and files them to shavings.) [45]

MIME
(who has sat down rather to one side, watches Siegfried at work.)

You're doing it wrong!
There is the solder,
prepared, melted and hot.

Was machst du denn da?
Nimm doch die Löte:
den Brei braut' ich schon längst.

SIEGFRIED

Off with your trash!
I need it not.
No solder patches my sword.

Fort mit dem Brei!
Ich brauch' ihn nicht:
mit Bappe back' ich kein Schwert!

MIME

But the file is finished,
the rasp is ruined!
You're filing the steel to splinters!

Du zerfeilst die Feile,
zerreibst die Raspel:
wie willst du den Stahl zerstampfen?

SIEGFRIED

It must be splintered
and ground into shreds;
what is broken, this way I mend.

Zersponnen muss ich
in Späne ihn sehn:
was entzwei ist, zwing ich mir so.

(He goes on filing vigorously.) [45]

84

(aside) [17]

My skill is useless,	Hier hilft kein Kluger,
I see that now	das seh ich klar:
only his folly	hier hilft dem Dummen
can serve in his need!	die Dummheit allein!
See how he toils	Wie er sich rührt
with mighty strokes!	und mächtig regt!
He's shredded the steel,	Ihm schwindet der Stahl,
Yet he still keeps cool!	doch wird ihm nicht schwül!

(Siegfried has fanned the forge fire to its brightest glow.) [13a]

Though I grew as old [13b]	Nun ward ich so alt
as cave and wood,	wie Höhl' und Wald
no sight like this would I see.	und hab nicht so was gesehn!

(While Siegfried with furious energy goes on filing down the pieces of the sword, Mime sits still further away.)

He will forge that sword,	Mit dem Schwert gelingt's,
I see that now;	das lern ich wohl:
fearless, he will succeed. [50]	furchtlos fegt er's zu ganz.
The Wanderer's words were true! [13a]	Der Wand'rer wusst' es gut!
And I must hide [13b]	Wie berg ich nun
my fearful head,	mein banges Haupt?
or else it falls to the boy, [39]	Dem kühnen Knaben verfiel's,
if I can't teach him to fear!	lehrt' ihn nicht Fafner die Furcht!

(With increasing anxiety he leaps us, and cringes.) [21]

But woe to Mime!	Doch weh mir Armen!
That dragon is safe	Wie würgt' er den Wurm,
if he can teach the boy.	erführ' er das Fürchten von ihm?
Then how would I gain the ring? [6]	Wie erräng' er mir den Ring?
Accursed problem!	Verfluchte Klemme!
I'm caught in a trap	Da klebt' ich fest,
if I can't find some way	fänd' ich nicht klugen Rat,
by which Siegfried is bent to my will.	wie den Furchtlosen selbst ich bezwäng'.

(has filed down the pieces and put them in a melting pot which he now places on the forge fire.)

Hey, Mime! Tell me	He, Mime! Geschwind!
the name of the sword	Wie heisst das Schwert,
which I have filed into pieces. [27]	das ich in Späne zersponnen?

(gives a start, and turns to Siegfried.)

Notung, that is	Notung nennt sich
the name of the sword:	das neidliche Schwert:
for your mother told me its name.	deine Mutter gab mir die Mär.

[45]

(during the following blows up the fire with the bellows.)

Notung! Notung! [27b]	Notung! Notung!
Sword of my need!	Neidliches Schwert!
What mighty blow once broke you?	Was musstest du zerspringen?
I've filed to splinters	Zu Spreu nun schuf ich
your shining steel;	die scharfe Pracht,
the fire has melted and fused them.	im Tiegel brat ich die Späne.
Hoho! Hoho!	Hoho! Hoho!
Hohi! Hohi! Hoho!	Hohei! Hohei! Hoho!
Bellows, blow!	Blase, Balg!
Brighten the glow! [51]	Blase die Glut!
Wild in woodlands	Wild im Walde
grew that tree	wuchs ein Baum,
I felled in the forest glade;	den hab ich im First gefällt:
I burnt to ashes	die braune Esche
branches and trunk;	brannt' ich zur Kohl',
on the hearth it lies in a heap.	auf dem Herd nun liegt sie gehäuft.

Hoho! Hoho!
Hohi! Hohi! Hoho!
Bellows, blow!
Brighten the glow!

The blackened charcoal
so bravely burns;
how bright and fair its glow!
A shower of sparks
is shooting on high:
Hohi! Hoho! Hohi!
and fuses the splintered steel.
Hoho! Hoho!
Hohi! Hohi! Hoho!
Bellows, blow!
Brighten the glow!

Hoho! Hoho!
Hohei! Hohei! Hoho!
Blase, Balg!
Blase die Glut!

Des Baumes Kohle,
wie brennt sie kühn;
wie glüht sie hell und hehr!
In springenden Funken
sprühet sie auf:
Hohei! Hohei! Hohei!
zerschmilzt mir des Stahles Spreu.
Hoho! Hoho!
Hohei! Hohei! Hoho!
Blase, Balg!
Blase die Glut!

MIME
(still to himself, sitting apart)

The sword will be forged
and Fafner conquered:
all that I can clearly foresee.
Gold and ring
will pass to the boy:
can I capture them both for me?
By wit and guile
I must obtain them,
and save my head as well.

Er schmiedet das Schwert
und Fafner fällt er:
das seh ich nun deutlich voraus.
Hort und Ring
erringt er im Harst:
[6]   wie erwerb ich mir den Gewinn?
[17]   Mit Witz und List
gewinn' ich beides
und berge heil mein Haupt.

SIEGFRIED
(still at the bellows)

Hoho! Hoho!
Hohi! Hohi! Hohi!

[27a]   Hoho! Hoho!
Hohei! Hohei! Hohei!

MIME
(downstage, to himself) [20]

After the fight he'll be tired,
and I'll quench his thirst with a drink.
From roots of flowers
that I have gathered
I'll make a dangerous drink.
If he tastes but one drop
of my potion,
sound sleep follows at once.
Then I'll seize that weapon,
the sword that he's forging;
I'll simply chop off his head;
then mine are the ring and the gold.

Rang er sich müd mit dem Wurm,
von der Müh' erlab' ihn ein Trunk:
[42]   aus würz'gen Säften,
die ich gesammelt,
brau ich den Trank für ihn;
wenig Tropfen nur
braucht er zu trinken,
[27]   sinnlos sinkt er in Schlaf.
Mit der eignen Waffe,
die er sich gewonnen,
räum ich ihn leicht aus dem Weg,
erlange mir Ring und Hort.

(He rubs his hands in glee.)

Hey, wise old Wanderer,
am I so dull?
Do you not approve
my crafty plan?
Have I found
my path to power?

Hei! Weiser Wand'rer!
Dünkt' ich dich dumm?
[17]   Wie gefällt dir nun
mein feiner Witz?
Fand ich mir wohl
Rat und Ruh?

SIEGFRIED

Notung! Notung!
Sword of my need!
I smelt your shining steel!
The fiery stream
must fill this mould.

[27b]   Notung! Notung!
Neidliches Schwert!
Nun schmolz deines Stahles Spreu!
[51]   Im eignen Schweisse
schwimmst du nun.

(He pours the glowing contents of the melting-pot into a mould, which he holds aloft.) [46]
And now you are shaped as my sword!   Bald schwing ich dich als mein Schwert!
(He plunges the mould into the water-trough; steam and loud hissing arise as it cools.)

In the water flowed	In das Wasser floss
a fiery flood:	ein Feuerfluss:
fury and hate	grimmiger Zorn
hissed from the blade!	zischt' ihm da auf!
That fire was soon quenched	Wie sehrend er floss,
by the fiery flood;	in des Wassers Flut
no more it stirs.	fliess er nicht mehr.
Strong, stubborn and hard,	Starr ward er und steif,
there lies my new-made sword.	herrisch der harte Stahl:
Burning blood [27]	heisses Blut doch
soon wets your blade!	fliesst ihm bald!

(He thrusts the steel into the forge fire, and works the bellows vigorously.) [51]

Once more I must heat you,	Nun schwitze noch einmal,
so I can shape you,	dass ich dich schweisse,
Notung, sword of my need!	Notung, neidliches Schwert!

(Mime has jumped up in delight, he fetches various vessels, and from them shakes spices and herbs into a cooking pot, which he tries to put on the hearth. Siegfried, watches Mime at work, as he carefully puts his pot on the fire from the other side of the hearth.)

But what is the booby	Was schafft der Tölpel
doing with the pot?	dort mit dem Topf?
I work with steel;	Brenn ich hier Stahl,
you're cooking soup there?	braust du dort Sudel?

MIME

The smith is put to shame:	Zuschanden kam ein Schmied;
the teacher is taught his craft.	den Lehrer sein Knabe lehrt:
When the master finds his skill has gone,	Mit der Kunst nun ist's beim Alten aus,
as cook he serves the child.	als Koch dient er dem Kind.
You make a broth of the steel;	Brennt es das Eisen zu Brei,
old Mime stirs his pot [49a]	aus Eiern braut
and makes soup.	der Alte ihm Sud.

(He goes on with his cooking.)

SIEGFRIED

Mime the craftsman	Mime, der Künstler,
turns to cooking; [17]	lernt jetzt kochen;
his anvil pleases him no more.	das Schmieden schmeckt ihm nicht mehr.
All the swords he made me	Seine Schwerter alle
broke into pieces;	hab ich zerschmissen;
what he cooks, I never will taste!	was er kocht, ich kost es ihm nicht!

(During what follows Siegfried takes the mould from the fire, breaks it, and lays the glowing steel on the anvil.)

What fear is [51]	Das Fürchten zu lernen,
I hope I shall soon discover.	will er mich führen;
Out there one dwells who can teach me;	ein Ferner soll es mich lehren:
seeing Mime can't help,	was am besten er kann,
he's no use to me;	mir bringt er's nicht bei;
whatever he does, he does badly!	als Stümper besteht er in allem!

(during the forging)

Hoho! Hoho! Hohi!	Hoho! Hoho! Hohei!
Forge me, my hammer,	Schmiede, mein Hammer,
a hard strong sword!	ein hartes Schwert!
Hoho! Hahi!	Hoho! Hahei!
Hoho! Hahi!	Hoho! Hahei!
Your steely blue	Einst färbt Blut
once flowed with blood;	dein falbes Blau;
its ruddy trickling	sein rotes Rieseln
reddened my blade;	rötete dich:
cold laughter you gave,	kalt lachtest du da,
the warm blood cooled on your blade!	das warme lecktest du kühl!
Hiaho, haha,	Heiaho! Haha!
Hahiaha!	Haheiaha!
But now with fire	Nun hat die Glut
you redly gleam,	dich rot geglüht;
and your weakness yields	deine weiche Härte
to my hammer's blow.	dem Hammer weicht:

Angry sparks you are showering
on me who conquer your pride!
  Hiaho! Hiaho!
  Hiahohoho!
  Hahi!

zornig sprühst du mir Funken,
dass ich dich Spröden gezähmt!
  Heiaho! Heiaho!
  Heiahohoho!
  Hahei!

[46]

MIME
(*aside*)

He's forging a bright, sharp sword.
  Fafner will feel it
  and meet his death.
I've brewed a deadly drink;
  Siegfried will follow
  when Fafner's dead.
My skill will gain me the prize;
ring and gold will be mine!

Er schafft sich ein scharfes Schwert,
  Fafner zu fällen,
  der Zwerge Feind:
ich braut' ein Truggetränk,
  Siegfried zu fangen,
  dem Fafner fiel.
Gelingen muss mir die List;
lachen muss mir der Lohn!

(*During what follows, he is busy pouring the contents of the pot into a flask.*)

SIEGFRIED

Hoho! Hoho!
Hahi!
  Forge me, my hammer,
  a hard strong sword!
Hoho! Hahi!
Hahi! Hoho!
This cheerful sparkling
  delights my heart;
  this flash of anger
  suits well my blade.
Now you laugh at your lord,
though you pretend to be grim!
  Hiaho, haha,
  haheiaha
Both heat and hammer
  serve me well;
  with sturdy strokes
  I beat you straight.
Now banish your blush of shame,
and be as cold and hard as you can.
  Hiaho! Hiaho!
  Hiahohoho!
  Hiah!

Hoho! Hoho!
Hahei!
  Schmiede, mein Hammer,
  ein hartes Schwert!
Hoho! Hahei!
Hahei! Hoho!
Der frohen Funken,
  wie freu ich mich;
  es ziert den Kühnen
  des Zornes Kraft:
lustig lachst du mich an,
stellst du auch grimm dich und gram!
  Heiaho, haha,
  haheiaha!
Durch Glut und Hammer
  glückt' es mir;
  mit starken Schlägen
  streckt' ich dich:
Nun schwinde die rote Scham;
werde kalt und hart, wie du kannst.
  Heiaho! Heiaho!
  Heiahohoho!
  Heiah!

(*He swings the steel and plunges it into the water-trough. He laughs at the loud sizzling. While Siegfried fastens the forged blade into a hilt, Mime fusses about with his flask downstage.*) [17]

MIME

Once my brother forged   [50]
  a bright shining ring,
  and in it he worked
  a powerful spell.   [13a]
That shining gold
  will belong to me,
  soon I will control it.
I'm master now!

Den der Bruder schuf,
  den schimmernden Reif,
  in den er gezaubert
  zwingende Kraft,
das helle Gold,
  das zum Herrscher macht,
  ihn hab ich gewonnen!
Ich walte sein!

(*While Siegfried is tapping with a small hammer and sharpening and filing, Mime skips about vivaciously, with increasing glee.*) [17, 50]

Alberich too,
  who made me his slave,
  will bend his knee
  and beg for my grace;
as Nibelung prince,
  all will obey me;
  that Niblung band
  will bow to me!
And the dwarf they despised

Alberich selbst,
  der einst mich band,
  zur Zwergenfrone
  zwing ich ihn nun;
als Niblungenfürst
  fahr ich darnieder;
  gehorchen soll mir
  alles Heer!
Der verachtete Zwerg,

they will treat as a king!	[17]	wie wird er geehrt!
All the heroes and gods		Zu dem Horte hin drängt sich
will respect my gold;		Gott und Held:

(with ever more lively gestures)

the world will cower	vor meinem Nicken
when I command;	neigt sich die Welt,
they'll beg my favour,	vor meinem Zorne
fearing my frown!	zittert sie hin!
I'll work no longer;	Dann wahrlich müht sich
Mime will rule.	Mime nicht mehr:
For me they'll labour,	ihm schaffen andre
to make me rich.	den ew'gen Schatz,
Mime the conqueror,	Mime, der kühne,
Mime is king now,	Mime ist König,
prince of the Niblungs,	Fürst der Alben,
lord of the world!	Walter des Alls!
Hi! Mime, you fortunate smith!	Hei, Mime: Wie glückte dir das!
Oh who could believe such luck!	Wer hätte wohl das gedacht?

SIEGFRIED

(during Mime's song has given the final blows to flatten the rivets on the hilt. He picks up the sword.)

Notung! Notung!	[27b]	Notung! Notung!
Sword of my need!		Neidliches Schwert!
You are fixed again firm in the hilt.		Jetzt haftest du wieder im Heft.
Snapped in two,	Warst du entzwei,
once more you are whole;	ich zwang dich zu ganz;
no stroke again shall ever smash you.	kein Schlag soll nun dich mehr zerschlagen.
You broke when my father	Dem sterbenden Vater
was doomed to death;	zersprang der Stahl,
his living son	der lebende Sohn
forged you again:	schuf ihn neu:
for me now you laugh and shine,	nun lacht ihm sein heller Schein,
and your gleaming edge will be keen.	seine Schärfe schneidet ihm hart.

(brandishing the sword)

Notung! Notung!		Notung! Notung!
Sword of my need!	[27]	Neidliches Schwert!
To life once more I have waked you.		Zum Leben weckt' ich dich wieder.
You lay there	Tot lagst du
so cold and dead,	in Trümmern dort,
but shine now defiant and fair.	jetzt leuchtest du trotzig und hehr.
Let every traitor	Zeige den Schächern
quail at your gleam!	nun deinen Schein!
Strike at the false one,	Schlage den Falschen,
strike at the rogue!	fälle den Schelm!
See, Mime, you smith:	Schau, Mime, du Schmied:

(He raises the sword to strike.)

| so strong is Siegfried's sword! | [46] So schneidet Siegfrieds Schwert! |

He strikes the anvil, which splits from top to bottom and falls apart with a great crash. Mime, who has jumped up on to a stool in ecstasy, falls off in fright and lands on the ground on his bottom. Jubilantly, Siegfried holds the sword aloft. The curtain falls.

Act Two

In the depths of the forest. Upstage is the mouth of a cave. The ground rises towards centre stage, where it forms a small knoll; from there it descends to the cave, so that only the top part of its mouth is visible to the audience. Through the trees, to the left, a rough cliff can be seen. It is dark night, at its darkest towards the back, where at first the audience can distinguish nothing. [52, 21, 6, 23, 22, 5x]

Scene One. *Alberich is stationed at the cliff-face, gloomily brooding.* [52]

ALBERICH

In gloomy night   [22]   In Wald und Nacht
by Fafner's cave I wait,   vor Neidhöhl' halt ich Wacht:
  my ears alert,   es lauscht mein Ohr,
keeping careful watch.   mühvoll lugt mein Aug'.
  Fateful day,   Banger Tag,
when will you break?   bebst du schon auf?
When will the dawn   Dämmerst du dort
  drive this dark away?   durch das Dunkel her?

(A stormy wind blows out of the forest on the right from where a bluish gleam also shines.) [36b]

Is a light glittering there?   Welcher Glanz zittert dort auf?
  Nearer and nearer   Näher schimmert
  it seems to shine;   ein heller Schein;
it runs like a fiery steed,   es rennt wie ein leuchtendes Ross,
  breaks through the wood,   bricht durch den Wald
  rushing this way.   brausend daher.
Can it be him I'm waiting for, Naht schon des Wurmes Würger?
author of Fafner's death?   Ist's schon, der Fafner fällt?

(The wind subsides; the gleam fades away.) [23]

The light has gone;   [52] Das Licht erlischt,
the glow fades from my sight. der Glanz barg sich dem Blick:
  Night and darkness!   Nacht ist's wieder.

(The Wanderer enters from the wood, and stops opposite Alberich.) [23]

Who comes there, lighting the shadows? [22] Wer naht dort schimmernd im Schatten?

WANDERER

To Neidhöhle   Zur Neidhöhle
by night I have come: fuhr ich bei Nacht:
who is hid in the darkness there? wen gewahr ich im Dunkel dort?

(As if through a sudden gap in the clouds, the moonlight breaks through and lights the Wanderer's face.) [8]

ALBERICH

(recognizes the Wanderer, flinches in fear, but then instantly breaks out in rage.)

You dare show yourself here?   Du selbst lässt dich hier sehn?
  What brings you here?   Was willst du hier?
  Out of my sight!   Fort, aus dem Weg!
Go elsewhere, shameless thief!   Von dannen, schamloser Dieb!

WANDERER
(calmly)

Black-Alberich,   Schwarz-Alberich,
  lurking here?   schweifst du hier?
Watching over Fafner's hoard?   Hütest du Fafners Haus?

ALBERICH

Driven by your greed   Jagst du auf neue
  to new evil deeds?   Neidtat umher?
Go on your way,   Weile nicht hier,
  take yourself elsewhere!   weiche von hinnen!
Too long we have suffered,   Genug des Truges
tricked by your scheming and lies. tränkte die Stätte mit Not.
  So, you traitor,   Drum, du Frecher,
leave us in peace!   lass sie jetzt frei!

The Wanderer watches,
takes no action.
Who dares to bar the Wanderer's way?

[49a] Zu schauen kam ich,
       nicht zu schaffen:
[49b] Wer wehrte mir Wandrers Fahrt?

ALBERICH
(*laughs maliciously*)

You false, infamous schemer!
I am not so stupid
as once you found me,
when you and Loge tricked me.
It's not so easy
again to capture my treasure!
Beware! I am warned,
wise to your schemes.
I know your weakness;
nothing is hid from the Niblung.
My stolen treasure
saved you from ruin;
my ring paid
for the giants' work,
who built that hall where you rule.
The terms of that bargain,
all that you swore then,
are graved for ever more
on that spear you hold in your hand.
You dare not
ever take back by force
that fee you paid to the giants:
for if you tried it
you would break the bond,
and in your hand
the shaft of your spear,
so mighty, would snap like a straw!

Du Rat wütender Ränke!
Wär' ich dir zulieb,
doch noch dumm wie damals,
als du mich Blöden bandest,
wie leicht geriet' es,
[36a] den Ring mir nochmals zu rauben!
Hab Acht! Deine Kunst
kenne ich wohl;
doch wo du schwach bist,
blieb mir auch nicht verschwiegen.
Mit meinen Schätzen
zahltest du Schulden;
mein Ring lohnte
[8] der Riesen Müh',
[9a] die deine Burg dir gebaut.
Was mit den trotzigen
einst du vertragen,
des Runen wahrt noch heut
deines Speeres herrischer Schaft.
[15] Nicht du darfst,
      was als Zoll du gezahlt,
den Riesen wieder entreissen:
du selbst zerspelltest
deines Speeres Schaft;
in deiner Hand
der herrische Stab,
[52] der starke, zerstiebte wie Spreu!

Yet no bonds nor graven bargains
bound evil
Alberich to me:
By force, I bent your will to mine;
my spear brings victory in war.

[49a] Durch Vertrages Treuerunen
      band er dich
[9a] Bösen mir nicht:
dich beugt' er mir durch seine Kraft;
zum Krieg drum wahr ich ihn wohl.

ALBERICH

How grand you sound,
how proudly you stand there,
and yet in your heart there is fear!
The dragon must die,
for, by my curse
on the gold, I've doomed him:
then who shall inherit?
Will the glittering gold
to the Niblung belong once again?
That thought gives you endless torment?
Just wait till I grasp
the ring in my hand.
I'm not a foolish giant.
I'll use that magic spell:
till you and your heroes
tremble before me!
Alberich's army
conquers Walhall's height:
the world then shall be mine!

[22] Wie stolz du dräust
      in trotziger Stärke,
[23] und wie dir's im Busen doch bangt!
Verfallen dem Tod
durch meinen Fluch
ist des Hortes Hüter:
Wer wird ihn beerben?
Wird der neidliche Hort
dem Niblungen wieder gehören?
Das sehrt dich mit ew'ger Sorge!
Denn fass ich ihn wieder
einst in der Faust,
anders als dumme Riesen
[6] üb ich des Ringes Kraft:
dann zittre der Helden
ewiger Hüter!
[5x] Walhalls Höhen
stürm ich mit Hellas Heer:
[8b, 13a, 6] der Welt walte dann ich!

WANDERER
(calmly)

Though I know what you plan, [8a]	Deinen Sinn kenn' ich wohl;
I care not at all,	doch sorgt er mich nicht.
The ring's new master,	Des Ringes waltet,
he shall be lord.	wer ihn gewinnt.

ALBERICH

How darkly you tell me	Wie dunkel sprichst du,
what so clearly I know! [27]	was ich deutlich doch weiss!
A hero helps you,	An Heldensöhne
that's what you plan,	hält sich dein Trotz,
that son who was born from your blood?	die traut deinem Blute entblüht.
Have you not raised up a hero	Pflegst du wohl eines Knaben,
in hopes that he will gather	der klug die Frucht dir pflücke,
that fruit you dare not pluck?	[36a]die du nicht brechen darfst?

WANDERER

Not my plan!	Mit mir nicht,
Struggle with Mime;	hadre mit Mime:
your brother threatens your hopes:	dein Bruder bringt dir Gefahr;
to this place he's leading the boy,	einen Knaben führt er daher,
and Fafner will fall to him.	der Fafner ihm fällen soll.
He knows naught of me,	Nichts weiss der von mir;
but Mime urges him on.	der Niblung nützt ihn für sich.
So mark my words, good friend:	Drum sag ich dir, Gesell,
you may act as you please!	tue frei, wie dir's frommt!

(Alberich gestures to show his extreme curiosity.) [19]

Take my advice,	Höre mich wohl,
be on your guard!	sei auf der Hut!
The boy knows naught of the ring,	Nicht kennt der Knabe den Ring;
till Mime tells him the tale.	doch Mime kundet ihn aus.

ALBERICH
(eagerly) [19]

And will you play no part at all?	Deine Hand hieltest du vom Hort?

WANDERER

Since I love him,	Wen ich liebe,
I must refuse to help him;	lass ich für sich gewähren;
he stands or he falls	er steh' oder fall',
unhelped by me:	sein Herr ist er:
gods rely only on heroes.	Helden nur können mir frommen.

ALBERICH

With only Mime	Mit Mime räng' ich
I strive for the ring?	allein um den Ring?

WANDERER

Only you and he	Ausser dir begehrt er
have plans on the gold.	einzig das Gold.

ALBERICH

And yet I cannot make it my own?	Und dennoch gewänn' ich ihn nicht?

WANDERER
(quietly drawing nearer)

A hero nears	Ein Helde naht,
to rescue the hoard;	den Hort zu befrein;
two Nibelungs long for the gold:	zwei Niblungen geizen das Gold;
Fafner falls, [21]	Fafner fällt,
he who guards the ring.	der den Ring bewacht:
When it's seized — luck to the winner!	wer ihn rafft, hat ihn gewonnen.
Would you know more?	Willst du noch mehr?
There Fafner lies:	Dort liegt der Wurm.

(He turns towards the cave.) [52]

why not warn him of death?　　　　Warnst du ihn vor dem Tod,
Maybe he'll give you the ring.　　　willig wohl liess' er den Tand.
I'll wake him up with my call.　　　Ich selber weck ihn dir auf.
(*He takes up a position on the knoll in front of the cave, and calls into it.*) [21]
Fafner! Fafner!　　　　　　　　Fafner! Fafner!
You dragon, wake!　　　　　　　Erwache, Wurm!

ALBERICH
(*excited and astonished, to himself*)

Has he lost his senses?　　　　　Was beginnt der Wilde?
Can it be mine now?　　　　　　Gönnt er mir's wirklich?
(*From the dark depths at the back Fafner's voice is heard through a powerful loudspeaker.*)

FAFNER

Who wakes me from sleep?　　　　Wer stört mir den Schlaf?

WANDERER
(*facing the cave*)

A friend has arrived here,　　　　Gekommen ist einer,
　warning of danger;　　　　　　Not dir zu künden:
he has a plan to save you.　　　　er lohnt dir's mit dem Leben,
Will you reward his help　　　　　lohnst du das Leben ihm
with the treasure you are guarding?　mit dem Horte, den du hütest?
(*He inclines his ear towards the cave, listening.*)

FAFNER

What would he?　　　　　　　　Was will er?

ALBERICH
(*has joined the Wanderer, and calls into the cave.*)

Waken, Fafner!　　　　　　　　Wache, Fafner!
Dragon, awake!　　　　　　　　Wache, du Wurm!
A valiant hero comes　　　　　　Ein starker Helde naht,
to try his strength against yours.　dich Heil'gen will er bestehn.

FAFNER

Then food is near.　　　　　[52]　Mich hungert sein.

WANDERER

Bold is his youthful heart,　　[27]　Kühn is des Kindes Kraft,
sharp-edged is his sword.　　　　scharf schneidet sein Schwert.

ALBERICH

The golden ring　　　　　　[6]　Den golden Reif
　that's all he wants:　　　　　geizt er allein:
just give that ring to me,　　[5x]　Lass mir den Ring zum Lohn,
　and then he won't fight.　　　　so wend ich den Streit;
You keep all the rest,　　　　　du wahrest den Hort
and live your life in peace!　　　und ruhig lebst du lang!

FAFNER

I'll keep what I hold —　　　[52]　Ich lieg und besitz —
(*yawning*)
let me slumber!　　　　　　　　lasst mich schlafen!

WANDERER
(*laughs aloud, and turns back to Alberich.*)

Well, Alberich! That scheme failed!　[6]　Nun, Alberich, das schlug fehl.
Yet call me not a rogue!　　　　Doch schilt mich nicht mehr Schelm!
Still more I'll tell you;　　　　　Dies eine, rat ich,
　heed my advice!　　　　　　　achte noch wohl!
(*approaching him confidentially*) [1b]
All things go their appointed way;　Alles ist nach seiner Art,
their course you cannot alter.　　an ihr wirst du nichts ändern.
I'll leave you alone here;　　　　Ich lass dir die Stätte,
　be on your guard!　　　　　　stelle dich fest!

Beware of Mime, your brother; he is your kind, and you understand him.	Versuch's mit Mime, dem Bruder, der Art ja versiehst du dich besser.

(turning to go) [9a]

But stranger things you'll learn in good time!	Was anders ist, das lerne nun auch!

(He disappears into the forest. The storm wind rises, the bright gleam breaks out; then both quickly subside.) [27, 49a]

ALBERICH
(gazes after the Wanderer as he rides away.)

He rides on his way, on fiery steed, and leaves me to care and shame. Yet laugh away, you light-spirited, self-worshipping clan of immortals! One day I shall see you all fade! So long as gold reflects the light, here a wise one will watch: watching, waiting to strike!	Da reitet er hin auf lichtem Ross [44a]mich lässt er in Sorg' und Spott. Doch lacht nur zu, ihr leichtsinniges, lustgieriges [23] Göttergelichter! Euch seh ich noch alle vergehn! Solang das Gold am Lichte glänzt, hält ein Wissender Wacht. [22] Trügen wird euch sein Trotz! [52]

(He slips aside into the cleft in the rocks. The stage remains empty. Day dawns.) [52]

Scene Two. *As day breaks, Mime and Siegfried enter. Siegfried is wearing the sword on a belt of rope. Mime spies out the land; lastly he investigates the backstage area which remains in deep shadow even while, later on, the knoll in the middle foreground is lit up increasingly brightly by the sun; then he addresses Siegfried.* [51, 47, 17, 43]

MIME

We go no further! Here's the place!	Wir sind zur Stelle! Bleib hier stehn!

SIEGFRIED
(sits down under a large lime tree and gazes around.)

Here, then, shall this fear be taught me? So far I've let you lead me; for the whole night long we've wandered through this dark wood, side by side. Mime, I need you no longer! If I don't learn what I've come to find, alone I shall go onward; from Mime, I must be free!	Hier soll ich das Fürchten lernen? Fern hast du mich geleitet: eine volle Nacht im Walde. selbander wandertern wir. Nun sollst du, Mime, mich meiden! Lern ich hier nicht, was ich lernen muss, allein zieh ich dann weiter: dich endlich werd ich da los!

MIME
(sits down opposite Siegfried, where he can keep one eye on the cave.) [13b]

Child, believe me, if you do not learn to fear today, no other place, no other time, can ever teach you fear. Look back there; do you see that dreadful cave? Deep inside there lives a cruel dragon, terribly big, and savage and fierce. As soon as he sees you he'll open his jaws, to eat you whole. One single gulp — the brute will gobble you down!	Glaube, Liebster, lernst du heut und hier das Fürchten nicht, an andrem Ort, zu andrer Zeit schwerlich erfährst du's je. Siehst du dort den dunklen Höhlenschlund? Darin wohnt ein greulich wilder Wurm: [52] ummassen grimmig ist er und gross; ein schrecklicher Rachen reisst sich ihm auf; mit Haut und Haar auf einen Happ verschlingt der Schlimme dich wohl.

Well then, in order to stop him,
I'll close up his jaws with my sword.

Gut ist's, den Schlund ihm zu schliessen;
drum biet ich mich nicht dem Gebiss.

MIME

Poisonous foam
he will pour from his mouth;
if you are splashed
by one single drop,
it shrivels your body and bones.

Giftig giesst sich
ein Geifer ihm aus:
wen mit des Speichels
Schweiss er bespeit,
dem schwinden wohl Fleisch und Gebein.

SIEGFRIED

But that poisonous foam cannot harm me,
if I step neatly aside.

Dass des Geifers Gift mich nicht sehre,
weich ich zur Seite dem Wurm.

MIME

A scaly tail
he lashes around:
and if you should be caught,
he'll coil it tight;
your bones will be broken like glass!

Ein Schlangenschweif
schlägt sich ihm auf:
wen er damit umschlingt
und fest umschliesst,
dem brechen die Glieder wie Glas!

SIEGFRIED

Then that scaly tail must not catch me;

I'll have to watch it with care.
But tell me one thing:
has the brute a heart?

Vor des Schweifes Schwang mich zu
wahren,
halt' ich den Argen im Aug'.
[33] Doch heisse mich das:
hat der Wurm ein Herz?

MIME

A merciless, cruel heart.

[52] Ein grimmiges, hartes Herz!

SIEGFRIED

And is that heart
in the usual place,
at the left of his breast?

Das sitzt ihm doch,
wo es jedem schlägt,
[13b]trag' es Mann oder Tier?

MIME

Of course; dragons
have hearts like men.
Does your heart begin to feel fear?

Gewiss, Knabe,
da führt's auch der Wurm.
Jetzt kommt dir das Fürchten wohl an?

SIEGFRIED
(*who has stretched out carelessly, quickly sits up.*)

Notung! Notung
I'll thrust in that heart!
In that way may fear be taught me?
Oh, you're stupid!
Have you brought me
all this way
to teach me that?
Mime, be off and leave me;
since fear I shall never learn here.

[27b] Notung stoss ich
dem Stolzen ins Herz!
Soll das etwa Fürchten heissen?
[47] He, du Alter!
Ist das alles,
was deine List
mich lehren kann?
Fahr deines Weges dann weiter;
das Fürchten lern ich hier nicht.

MIME

Just wait a while!
You think I've told you
trifling and empty tales:
but Fafner
you must see for yourself;
for Fafner can teach you to fear.
When your eyes grow dim,
your body grows weak,
when trembling shudders
fill your heart,

[13b] Wart es nur ab!
Was ich dir sage,
dünke dich tauber Schall:
ihn selber musst du
hören und sehn,
die Sinne vergehn dir dann schon!
[43] Wenn dein Blick verschwimmt,
der Boden dir schwankt,
im Busen bang
[52] dein Herz erbebt:

you'll thank the dwarf who has brought you,
be glad of Mime's love.

dann dankst du mir, der dich führte,
gedenkst, wie Mime dich liebt.

SIEGFRIED

You must not love me!
Did you not hear?
I hate the sight of you!
Leave me alone:
I'll hear no more talk about love;
don't dare to love me again!
   That shuffling and slinking,
those eyelids blinking —
how long must I
endure the sight?
When shall I be rid of this fool?

Du sollst mich nicht lieben!
Sagt' ich dir's nicht?
Fort aus den Augen mir!
Lass mich allein:
sonst halt ich's hier länger nicht aus,
fängst du von Liebe gar an!
[17] Das eklige Nicken
und Augenzwicken,
wann endlich soll ich's
nicht mehr sehn,
wann werd ich den Albernen los?

MIME

I'll leave you now,
at the stream I'll cool myself.
   Wait by the cave;
soon, when the sun is in the sky,
watch for the dragon.
From his cave he'll slowly emerge,
wind his way
past this place,
to reach the cooling stream there.

Ich lass dich schon.
Am Quell dort lagr' ich mich:
steh du nur hier;
steigt dann die Sonne zur Höh',
[21] merk auf den Wurm:
aus der Höhle wälzt er sich her,
hier vorbei
biegt er dann,
am Brunnen sich zu tränken.

SIEGFRIED
(laughing)

Mime, wait by the stream,
and let the dragon catch you there:
   I can wait here
till Fafner has found you,
then we can fight —
after you've been swallowed.
Or else, take my advice,
better not stay by the stream;
hurry away
as fast as you can,
and don't come back to me!

Mime, weilst du am Quell,
dahin lass ich den Wurm wohl gehn:
   Notung stoss ich
ihm erst in die Nieren,
wenn er dich selbst dort
[17] mit weggesoffen.
Darum, hör meinen Rat,
raste nicht dort am Quell;
kehre dich weg,
so weit du kannst,
und komm nie mehr zu mir!

MIME

When after the fight
you need refreshment,
won't you be glad to see me?

Nach freislichem Streit
dich zu erfrischen,
wirst du mir wohl nicht wehren?

(Siegfried shoos him away.)

Call for my help
if you should need me.

Rufe mich auch,
darbst du des Rates —

(Siegfried impatiently repeats the gesture.)

Let me know when your fear has been learnt.

oder wenn dir das Fürchten gefällt.

(Siegfried gets up, and drives Mime away with angry gestures.) [47]

MIME
(to himself, as he goes) [17]

Fafner and Siegfried,
Siegfried and Fafner —
if only each would kill the other!

Fafner und Siegfried,
Siegfried und Fafner —
O, brächten beide sich um!

(He disappears into the forest on the right.)

SIEGFRIED
(stretches himself out comfortably under the lime tree, and watches Mime's departure.)

So he's no father of mine:
that thought fills my heart with joy!

Dass der mein Vater nicht ist,
wie fühl ich mich drob so froh!

Now I delight	Nun erst gefällt mir
in this fair green wood;	der frische Wald;
I delight	nun erst lacht mir
in this glorious day,	der lustig Tag,
now I'm free from that loathsome dwarf.	da der Garstige von mir schied
and I shan't have to see him again!	und ich gar nicht ihn wiederseh!

(He falls into silent reverie.)

My father, how did he look?	Wie sah mein Vater wohl aus?
Why, of course, like his son!	Ha, gewiss, wie ich selbst!
If Mime had fathered a son,	[17] Denn wär' wo von Mime ein Sohn,
wouldn't he look	müsst' er nicht ganz
just like Mime?	Mime gleichen?
Shuffling and slinking,	Grade so garstig,
grizzled and gray,	griesig und grau,
small and crooked,	klein und krumm,
limping and hunchbacked,	höckrig und hinkend,
with ears that are drooping,	mit hängenden Ohren,
eyes that are bleary . . .	triefigen Augen —
Off with the imp!	Fort mit dem Alp!
I hope he's gone for good!	Ich mag ihn nicht mehr sehn.

(He leans back and looks up through the branches. Deep silence. Forest murmurs.) [31]

Could I but know	Aber — wie sah
what my mother was like!	meine Mutter wohl aus?
That's something	Das kann ich
I cannot imagine!	nun gar nicht mir denken!
Her eyes have shone	[31] Der Rehhindin gleich
with soft gentle light,	glänzten gewiss
like the eyes of the roedeer,	ihr hell schimmernde Augen,
only more lovely!	nur noch viel schöner!
In fear and grief she bore me,	Da bang sie mich geboren,
but why did she die through me?	warum aber starb sie da?
Must every human mother	Sterben die Menschenmütter
die when her children	an ihren Söhnen
come to the world?	alle dahin?
Sad the world must be then!	[48a] Traurig wäre das, traun!
Ah, how this son	[30a] Ach, möcht' ich Sohn
longs to see his mother!	meine Mutter sehen!
See my mother —	Meine Mutter —
who lived and died!	[11a] ein Menschenweib!

(He sighs gently and leans back further. Deep silence. The forest murmurs increase. Siegfried's attention is then caught by the song of the forest birds. He listens with growing interest to a bird in the branches above him.) [53]

You lovely woodbird,	Du holdes Vöglein!
how sweet is your song:	Dich hört ich noch nie:
here in the wood is your home?	bist du im Wald hier daheim?
I wish I could understand you!	Verstünd' ich sein süsses Stammeln,
I'm sure you've something to tell —	gewiss sagt' es mir was
perhaps of a loving mother?	vielleicht von der lieben Mutter?
A surly old dwarf	Ein zankender Zwerg
said to me once	hat mir erzählt,
that men could learn	der Vöglein Stammeln
the language of birds,	gut zu verstehn,
and know what they were saying,	dazu könnte man kommen.
How can I learn the tongue?	Wie das wohl möglich wär'?

(He reflects. His glance falls on a clump of reeds not far from the lime tree.)

Hey! Let me try —	Hei, ich versuch's,
pipe your notes	sing ihm nach:
on a reed, copy your chirping!	auf dem Rohr tön ich ihm ähnlich!
Your song I will echo,	Entrat ich der Worte,
mimic your warbling;	achte der Weise,
while your tune I am piping,	sing ich so seine Sprache,
perhaps I shall learn what you say!	versteh ich wohl auch, was er spricht.

(He runs to the stream nearby, cuts a reed with his sword, and quickly whittles a pipe from it. He listens again.) [54, 53]

He stops and waits:	Er schweigt und lauscht:

97

well, let me begin!   so schwatz ich denn los!

(He blows on the pipe, breaks off, cuts it again to improve it, pipes again, shakes his head, and cuts the pipe once more. He tries again, gets angry, pinches the reed with his hand, and makes another attempt. Then he gives up.) [53b]

Well, that's not right;	Das tönt nicht recht;
and this reed won't serve	auf dem Rohre taugt
to capture the lilt of your song.	die wonnige Weise mir nicht.
Woodbird, I think	Vöglein, mich dünkt,
I must be dull;	ich bleibe dumm:
from you I cannot learn.	von dir lernt sich's nicht leicht!

(He hears the bird again, and looks up at it.)

You put me to shame	Nun schäm ich mich gar
as you perch there and watch me;	vor dem schelmischen Lauscher:
you wait — and I cannot answer.	er lugt und kann nichts erlauschen.
Hey then! Then hear	Heida! So höre
the call of my horn.	nun auf mein Horn.

(He holds up the reed and tosses it far away.)

I can pipe no tune	Auf dem dummen Rohre
on a feeble reed.	gerät mir nichts.
But I'll play you	Einer Waldweise,
a tune on my horn,	wie ich sie kann,
a song that will ring through the wood-	der lustigen sollst du nun lauschen.
lands —	
a song that I hoped	Nach liebem Gesellen
might find me a friend:	lockt' ich mit ihr:
though no one heard me	nichts Bessres kam noch
but wolf and bear.	als Wolf und Bär.
Now let us see	Nun lass mich sehn,
who'll answer my call —	wen jetzt sie mir lockt:
the friend whom I'm longing to find?	[11a]ob das mir ein lieber Gesell?

He takes the silver horn and blows on it. At each long-sustained note he looks up expectantly at the bird. There is a stir in the background. Fafner, in the form of a huge, scaly dragon, has risen from his lair in the cave; he breaks through the undergrowth and drags himself up from below to the higher ground until the front part of his body rests on this, whereupon he utters a loud noise like a yawn. [45, 39, 21, 46] *Siegfried looks round, and fastens his astonished gaze on Fafner.*

Haha! At last with my call	Haha! Da hätte mein Lied
I have lured something lovely!	mir was Liebes erblasen!
What a pretty playmate I've found!	Du wärst mir ein saubrer Gesell!

FAFNER
(at the sight of Siegfried has paused on the knoll, and remains there.) [50]

Who is there?   Was ist da?

SIEGFRIED

Hi, so you're a beast	Ei, bist du ein Tier,
that can speak to me,	das zum Sprechen taugt,
perhaps you've some news to tell me?	wohl liess sich von dir was lernen?
Can you tell me	Hier kennt einer
what fear might be:	das Fürchten nicht:
are you prepared to teach me?	kann er's von dir erfahren?

FAFNER

You are far too bold!   Hast du Übermut?

SIEGFRIED

Bold, maybe far too bold,	Mut oder Übermut,
I know not!	was weiss ich!
I know that I will fight you,	Doch dir fahr ich zu Leibe,
if you can't teach me to fear.	lehrst du das Fürchten mich nicht!

FAFNER
(makes a laughing noise.)

Drink I wanted,   Trinken wollt' ich:

| now I have found food! | nun treff ich auf Frass! |

(He opens his jaws and shows his teeth.)

What a splendid array	Eine zierliche Fresse
of dazzling teeth,	zeigst du mir da,
glinting and glistening	lachende Zähne
within those jaws!	im Leckermaul!
Well, maybe it's wiser to close them:	Gut wär' es, den Schlund dir zu schliessen;
those jaws are open too wide.	dein Rachen reckt sich zu weit!

FAFNER

For idle chatter,	[52] Zu tauben Reden
far too wide;	taugt es schlecht:
but all the better	dich zu verschlingen,
for my meal.	frommt der Schlund.

(He threatens with his tail.)

SIEGFRIED

Oho! You cruel	Hoho! Du grausam
merciless brute!	grimmiger Kerl!
But I've no wish	Von dir verdaut sein
to be your breakfast.	dünkt mich übel:
Far better plan, I think,	rätlich und fromm doch scheint's,
to destroy you here on the spot.	du verrecktest hier ohne Frist.

FAFNER
(roaring)

| Pruh! Come, | Pruh! Komm, |
| insolent boy! | prahlendes Kind! |

SIEGFRIED

| Take care, growler! | Hab Acht, Brüller! |
| The boy draws near! | Der Prahler naht! |

(He draws his sword, springs toward Fafner, and stands in an attitude of defiance. Fafner drags himself further up the knoll and spits from his nostrils at Siegfried. Siegfried avoids the venom, leaps nearer, and stands to one side. Fafner tries to reach him with his tail. When Fafner has nearly caught Siegfried, the latter leaps with one bound over the dragon, and wounds him in the tail. Fafner roars, draws his tail back quickly, and rears up the front part of his body to throw its full weight on Siegfried, thus exposing his breast. Siegfried quickly notes the place of the heart and plunges his sword in there up to the hilt. Fafner rears up still higher in his pain, and sinks down on the wound, as Siegfried lets go of the sword and leaps to one side.)
[46, 21, 45, 52]

SIEGFRIED

| So there, merciless brute! | [52] Da lieg, neidischer Kerl: |
| Notung now has destroyed you! | Notung trägst du im Herzen! |

FAFNER
(in a weaker voice)

Who are you, youthful hero,	[22, 45, 52] Wer bist du, kühner Knabe,
who have pierced my breast?	der das Herz mir traf?
Who roused up your fearless heart	Wer reizte des Kindes Mut
to this murderous deed?	zu der mordlichen Tat?
And who told you to do	[23] Dein Hirn brütete nicht,
what you have done?	was du vollbracht.

SIEGFRIED

Not much have I learned;	[39] Viel weiss ich noch nicht,
I know not who I am;	noch nicht auch, wer ich bin.
but you roused me to kill you,	Mit dir mordlich zu ringen,
prompted my deed by your threat.	reiztest du selbst meinen Mut.

FAFNER

| So bold, youthful, and fearless, | Du helläugiger Knabe, |

unknown to yourself:
  now let me tell you
  whom you have killed.
The giants who ruled on the earth,
  Fasolt and Fafner,
the brothers, both have now fallen.
  For the cursed gold
  we gained from the gods,
I put Fasolt to death.
  In dragon shape,
  the treasure's guardian,
Fafner, the last of the giants,
falls at the hand of a boy.
  Guard yourself well,
  bold, fearless hero!
He who urged you on to this deed,
has planned next this bold hero's death.
  Mark how it ends then!

Recall my fate!

unkund deiner selbst,
  wen du gemordet,
  meld ich dir.
[12] Der Riesen ragend Geschlecht,
  Fasolt und Fafner,
[52] die Brüder, fielen nun beide.
[6] Um verfluchtes Gold,
  von Göttern vergabt,
  traf ich Fasolt zu Tod.
[21] Der nun als Wurm
  den Hort bewachte,
  Fafner, den letzten Riesen,
[46] fällte ein rosiger Held.
[22] Blicke nun hell,
  blühender Knabe;
  der dich Blinden reizte zur Tat,
  berät jetzt des Blühenden Tod!
[23] Merk, wie's endet!
     (dying)

Acht auf mich!

SIEGFRIED

Who was my father?
  Do you not know?
  Wisdom inspires you
  now you are dying:
maybe my name will tell you:
Siegfried, that is my name.

Woher ich stamme,
  rate mir noch;
  weise ja scheinst du,
  Wilder, im Sterben;
[39] rat es nach meinem Namen:
  Siegfried bin ich genannt.

FAFNER

Siegfried! . . .

[52] Siegfried! . . .
(He raises himself with a sigh, and expires.)

SIEGFRIED

The dead can tell no tidings.
  To life I'll be led
  by the light of my sword!
(Fafner, in dying, has rolled on his side. Siegfried draws the sword from his breast, and in doing so smears his hand with blood. He draws it back violently.) [46]
Like fire burns the blood!
(Involuntarily he puts his fingers to his mouth to suck the blood from them. As he gazes thoughtfully before him, his attention is caught increasingly by the song of the forest birds.) [51]
  Almost, it seems,
the woodbirds are speaking to me.
  Is it a spell
  that lies in the blood?
The woodbird's there again;
hark, he sings to me!

Zur Kunde taugt kein Toter.
  So leite mich denn
  mein lebendes Schwert!

Wie Feuer brennt das Blut!

  Ist mir doch fast,
als sprächen die Vöglein zu mir!
  Nützte mir das
  des Blutes Genuss?
  Das seltne Vöglein hier,
  horch, was singet es mir?

THE VOICE OF A WOODBIRD
(from the branches of the lime tree above Siegfried)

Hi! Siegfried inherits
  the Nibelung hoard;
  oh, there it is lying
  within that cave!
There is the Tarnhelm, whose magic
will serve him for glorious deeds;
and if he discovers the ring,
it will make him the lord of the world!

[53c, 53d] Hei! Siegfried gehört
  nun der Niblungen Hort!
  O fänd' in der Höhle
  den Hort er jetzt!
  Wollt' er den Tarnhelm gewinnen,
  der taugt' ihm zu wonniger Tat:
  doch wollt' er den Ring sich erraten,
  der macht' ihn zum Walter der Welt!

SIEGFRIED
(has listened enraptured and with bated breath)

Thanks, dearest woodbird,

Dank, liebes Vöglein,

100

for that advice!
I'll do as you say!
(*He turns, descends into the cave, and disappears from sight.*) [8a]

für deinen Rat!
Gern folg' ich dem Ruf!

Scene Three. *Mime slinks on, peering round timidly to assure himself that Fafner is dead. Simultaneously, Alberich emerges from the rocks on the other side. He observes Mime closely. Mime, seeing that Siegfried is no longer there, is going warily towards the cave at the back, when Alberich rushes forward and bars his way.*

ALBERICH

Hehe! Sly
and slippery knave,
where are you going?

Wohin schleichst du
eilig und schlau,
schlimmer Gesell?

MIME

Accursed brother,
I need you not!
What brings you here?

Verfluchter Bruder,
dich braucht' ich hier!
Was bringt dich her?

ALBERICH

Pestilent imp,
you'd steal my gold?
You covet my wealth?

Geizt es dich, Schelm,
nach meinem Gold?
Verlangst du mein Gut?

MIME

Do I disturb
a thief at his work?
Caught in the act?

Stör ich dich wohl
im stillen Geschäft,
wenn du hier stiehlst?

MIME

What I've achieved
through years of toil
shall not escape me.

Was ich erschwang
mit schwerer Müh',
soll mir nicht schwinden.

ALBERICH

Was it then you
who robbed the Rhine of its gold?
And was it your hand
that worked the spell in the ring?

Hast du dem Rhein
das Gold zum Ringe geraubt?
Erzeugtest du gar
den zähen Zauber im Reif?

MIME

Who made the Tarnhelm,
changing your shape at will?
Though you desired it,
that helm was made by me!

[18]   Wer schuf den Tarnhelm,
der die Gestalten tauscht?
Der sein bedurfte,
erdachtest du ihn wohl?

ALBERICH

You miserable bungler,
mine was the skill that inspired you!
My magic ring
showed how the helm could be made.

Was hättest du Stümper
[19] je wohl zu stampfen verstanden?
Der Zauberring
zwang mir den Zwerg erst zur Kunst.

MIME

And where is that ring?
You coward, the giants have seized it.
What you have lost,
I can gain by guile for myself.

Wo hast du den Ring?
Dir Zagem entrissen ihn Riesen!
Was du verlorst,
meine List erlangt es für mich.

ALBERICH

What the boy has won
will the miser lay hands on?
When the hero finds it,
that hero will keep his prize.

Mit des Knaben Tat
will der Knicker nun knausern?
Dir gehört sie gar nicht,
der Helle ist selbst ihr Herr!

I brought him up;	Ich zog ihn auf;
for my care now he can pay;	[17] für die Zucht zahlt er mir nun:
for years I slaved;	für Müh' und Last
my labours have won their reward!	erlauert' ich lang meinen Lohn!

ALBERICH

So you brought him up!	Für des Knaben Zucht
Does the beggarly,	will der knickrige
miserly knave	schäbige Knecht
think he's earned	keck und kühn
such pay? King would he be?	wohl gar König nun sein?
A flea-bitten dog	Dem räudigsten Hund
has better right	wäre der Ring
than you to the gold!	geratner als dir:
You'll never win,	nimmer erringst
you schemer, that mighty ring!	du, Rüpel, den Herrscherreif!

MIME
(scratches his head.)

Well, keep it then,	Behalt ihn denn
and guard it well,	und hüt ihn wohl,
that shining ring!	den hellen Reif!
You be lord:	Sei du Herr:
but still treat me as brother!	doch mich heisse auch Bruder!
Give me the Tarnhelm,	Um meines Tarnhelms
which I have made;	lustigen Tand
you keep the gold;	tausch ich dir:
then both are paid;	uns beiden taugt's,
each of us shares in the prize.	teilen die Beute wir so.

(He rubs his hands insinuatingly.)

ALBERICH
(laughing scornfully)

Share it with you?	Teilen mit dir?
And the Tarnhelm yours?	Und den Tarnhelm gar?
How sly you are!	Wie schlau du bist!
Not one moment's peace	Sicher schlief' ich
I'd have from your scheming!	niemals vor deinen Schlingen!

MIME
(beside himself)

You won't share them?	Selbst nicht tauschen?
You won't bargain?	Auch nicht teilen?
Nothing for me?	Leer soll ich gehn?
All must be yours?	Ganz ohne Lohn?

(screaming)

Not one thing will you leave me?	Gar nichts willst du mir lassen?

ALBERICH

Not a trinket!	[5x] Nichts von allem!
No, not a nail-head!	Nicht einen Nagel
All I deny you.	sollst du dir nehmen!

MIME
(in a towering rage)

Neither ring nor Tarnhelm	Weder Ring noch Tarnhelm
then shall reward you!	soll dir denn taugen!
I'll bargain no more!	Nicht teil ich nun mehr!
But I'll set against you	Gegen dich doch ruf ich
Siegfried himself	Siegfried zu Rat
with his cruel sword;	und des Recken Schwert;
that fearless boy	der rasche Held,
will pay you, brother of mine!	der richte, Brüderchen, dich!

(Siegfried appears in the background.)

Better turn round!
From the cavern, see where he comes!

[8a] Kehre dich um!
Aus der Höhle kommt er daher!

MIME

Trinkets and toys
he's sure to have found.

[6] Kindischen Tand
erkor er gewiss.

ALBERICH

He's found the Tarnhelm!

Den Tarnhelm hält er!

MIME

Also the ring!

Doch auch den Ring!

ALBERICH

Accurst! The ring!

Verflucht! Den Ring!

MIME
(*laughing maliciously*)

Get him to give you the ring, then!
Yet all the same I shall win it!

Lass ihn den Ring dir doch geben!
Ich will ihn mir schon gewinnen.
(*He slips back into the forest.*)

ALBERICH

Just wait, in the end
it will belong to its master!

Und doch seinem Herrn
soll er allein noch gehören!

(*He disappears among the rocks. During the foregoing, Siegfried has come slowly and thoughtfully from the cave with the Tarnhelm and ring. He regards his prizes meditatively, and pauses on the knoll in the middle of the stage, near the tree.*) [4]

SIEGFRIED

Tarnhelm and ring,
here they are:
I chose these things
from the hoard of heaped-up gold,
because the woodbird said I should.
I know not their use:
yet they'll serve to remind me —
these toys are the proof
that I conquered Fafner in fight;
but what fear is, that I've not learned!

Was ihr mir nützt,
weiss ich nicht,
[3] doch nahm ich euch
aus des Horts gehäuftem Gold,
weil guter Rat mir es riet.
So taug' eure Zier
als des Tages Zeuge,
es mahne der Tand,
[46] dass ich kämpfend Fafner erlegt,
[6] doch das Fürchten noch nicht gelernt!

(*He hangs the Tarnhelm from his belt and puts the ring on his finger. Dead silence. The forest murmurs increase. Siegfried again involuntarily becomes aware of the bird, to whose song he listens with bated breath.*)

VOICE OF THE WOODBIRD

Hi! Siegfried discovered
the Tarnhelm and ring!
Oh, let him beware
of the treacherous dwarf!
Oh, let Siegfried attend
to the crafty words Mime speaks!
What he really means
you will now understand,
made wise by the taste of the blood.

[53c] Hei! Siegfried gehört
nun der Helm und der Ring!
O traute er Mime,
dem Treulosen, nicht!
[53d]Hörte Siegfried nur scharf
auf des Schelmen Heuchlergered'!
Wie sein Herz es meint,
kann er Mime verstehn:
so nütz' ihm des Blutes Genuss.

(*Siegfried's demeanour and gestures show that he has understood the meaning of the bird's song. Seeing Mime approach, he remains motionless, leaning on his sword, observant and self-contained, in his place on the knoll, until the end of the following scene.*) [31]

MIME
(*slinks on and observes Siegfried from the foreground.*)

He broods, and he wonders
what he's found:
can he have met
a wily Wanderer,

Er sinnt und erwägt
der Beute Wert.
Weilte wohl hier
ein weiser Wand'rer,

roaming around,
advising the boy
with crafty talk and tales?
   Doubly sly
I'll have to be:
my cunningest snares
for him I shall lay,
and use my friendliest,
   falsest flattery
to capture this obstinate boy.

schweifte umher,
beschwatzte das Kind
mit list'ger Runen Rat?
   Zweifach schlau
sei nun der Zwerg:
Die listigste Schlinge
leg ich jetzt aus,
dass ich mit traulichem
   Truggerede
betöre das trotzige Kind.

(*He comes closer to Siegfried, welcoming him with wheedling gestures.*) [19]
   Be welcome, Siegfried!   [53c] Wilkommen, Siegfried!
   Say, my brave one,   [9a] Sag, du Kühner,
tell me if fear has been learned?   hast du das Fürchten gelernt?

SIEGFRIED

No teacher here could be found.   Den Lehrer fand ich noch nicht!
    [19]

MIME

But that cruel dragon —   Doch den Schlangenwurm,
I see that you've slain him?   [53c] du hast ihn erschlagen?
Did he not inspire you with fear?   Das war doch ein schlimmer Gesell?

SIEGFRIED

Though he was cruel and fierce,   So grimm und tückisch er war,
his death fills me with grief,   sein Tod grämt mich doch schier,
when far wickeder scoundrels   da viel üblere Schächer
live their lives still unpunished.   unerschlagen noch leben!
He who brought me here to fight   Der mich ihn morden hiess,
I hate far more than my foe!   den hass ich mehr als den Wurm!

MIME
(*very affectionately*)

   Now gently! For soon   Nur sachte! Nicht lange
you'll see me no more;   siehst du mich mehr:
   when death has closed   zum ew'gen Schlaf
your eyes in dark, eternal sleep!   schliess ich dir die Augen bald!
   For all that I needed   Wozu ich dich brauchte,
         (*as if praising him*)
you have achieved.   hast du vollbracht;
One thing but remains   jetzt will ich nur noch
for me to do: to win the treasure.   die Beute dir abgewinnen.
I think that task should be easy;   Mich dünkt, das soll mir gelingen;
you were never hard to deceive!   zu betören bist du ja leicht!
    [31]

SIEGFRIED

Deceive me, and then destroy me?   [53c]So sinnst du auf meinen Schaden?

MIME
(*astonished*)

   Is that what I said?   Wie, sagt' ich denn das?
      (*continuing tenderly*)
Siegfried! Hear me, my dear son!   Siegfried! Hör doch, mein Söhnchen!
You and all your kind   Dich und deine Art
in my heart I have hated;   hasst' ich immer von Herzen;
   and love played no part   aus Liebe erzog ich
in bringing you up.   dich Lästigen nicht:
The gold that's hid in Fafner's cave,   dem Horte in Fafners Hut,
that gold alone I sought to win.   dem Golde galt meine Müh'.
   (*as if he were promising him something pleasant*)
   Give me all   Gibst du mir das
that shining treasure, or else —   gutwillig nun nicht —

(as if he were ready to lay down his life for him)

Siegfried, my son,	Siegfried, mein Sohn,
you see it's quite clear,	das siehst du wohl selbst:

(with affectionate jocularity)

your life you'll just have to yield to me.   dein Leben musst du mir lassen!

[17, 19]

SIEGFRIED

Learning you hate me,		Dass du mich hassest,
brings me joy:	[53c, 31]	hör ich gern:
as for my life, why should I yield it?		doch auch mein Leben muss ich dir lassen?

MIME
(angrily)

That's not what I said!		Das sagt' ich doch nicht?
You have heard me all wrong!	[17]	Du verstehst mich ja falsch!

(He produces his flask, and takes evident pains to be convincing.)

After your fighting	Sieh, du bist müde
I know you're tired;	von harter Müh';
after such toil you are hot;	brünstig wohl brennt dir der Leib:
let me refresh you	dich zu erquicken
with cooling drink;	mit queckem Trank
Mime knew what you'd need.	säumt' ich Sorgender nicht.
While your sword you were forging.	Als dein Schwert du dir branntest,
I made some broth;	braut' ich den Sud;
drink but a drop,	trinkst du nun den,
and then I will seize your sword	gewinn ich dein trautes Schwert
and gain the gold as well!	und mit ihm Helm und Hort.

(He sniggers.)

[53c]

SIEGFRIED

So you'd seize my sword	So willst du mein Schwert
and all that it's won me;	und was ich erschwungen,
ring and Tarnhelm, you'd take them?	Ring und Beute, mir rauben?

MIME
(vehemently)

Why can't you hear what I say?		Was du doch falsch mich verstehst!
Tell me, am I not clear?		Stamml' ich, fasl' ich wohl gar?
I'm being so careful,	[19]	Die grösste Mühe
choosing my words,		geb ich mir doch,
and hiding my meaning,		mein heimliches Sinnen
trying to deceive you;		heuchelnd zu bergen,
and the foolish booby		und du dummer Bube
misinterprets my words.		deutest alles doch falsch!
Open your ears now,		Öffne die Ohren
and attend to me!		und vernimm genau:
Listen what Mime plans!		höre, was Mime meint!

(again very affectionately, with an evident effort to make himself understood)

Take this and drink it to cool you!	Hier nimm und trinke dir Labung!
My drinks pleased you before:	Mein Trank labte dich oft:
when you were thirsty,	tatst du auch unwirsch,
tired or hot,	stelltest dich arg:
I brought you drink;	was ich dir bot,
you grumbled, but you still drank it.	erbost auch, nahmst du doch immer.

SIEGFRIED
(without altering his expression)

A refreshing drink	Einen guten Trank
I should like:	hätt' ich gern:
but say how this one was brewed.	wie hast du diesen gebraut?

MIME

(gaily joking, as if describing the state of cheerful intoxication the brew would induce)

Hi! Just drink it;	Hei! So trink nur,
trust to my skill!	trau meiner Kunst!
And you'll be seized	In Nacht und Nebel
by sleep that you cannot resist:	sinken die Sinne dir bald:
you will sink unconscious,	ohne Wach' und Wissen
drugged, drowsy, and helpless.	[50] stracks streckst du die Glieder.
While you're asleep	Liegst du nun da,
I'll easily [13a]	leicht könnt' ich
steal the ring and the Tarnhelm.	die Beute nehmen und bergen:
But if once you should wake	doch erwachtest du je,
then from you	nirgends wär' ich
I'd never be safe,	sicher vor dir,
even as lord of the ring.	[50] hätt' ich selbst auch den Ring.
So with the sword [13a]	Drum mit dem Schwert,
that you made so sharp,	das so scharf du schufst,

(with a gesture of uncontrolled merriment)

I will just chop	hau ich dem Kind
your head right off;	den Kopf erst ab:
then I will be safe. I'll have the ring!	dann hab ich mir Ruh' und auch den Ring!

SIEGFRIED

While I'm sleeping you plan to kill me?	Im Schlafe willst du mich morden?

MIME

(in a furious rage)

To kill you? Did I say that?	Was möcht ich? Sagt' ich denn das?

(He makes an effort to assume his most charming tone of voice.)

I merely plan	Ich will dem Kind

(with meticulous clarity)

to chop your head right off!	nur den Kopf abhaun!

(with an expression of heartfelt anxiety for Siegfried's well-being)

Not only because [48b x]	Denn hasste ich dich
I hate you so;	auch nicht so sehr,
not only because	und hätt' ich des Schimpfs
I have suffered scorn and shame,	und der schändlichen Mühe
and long to take my vengeance;	auch nicht so viel zu rächen:

(gently)

but because I must destroy you.	aus dem Wege dich zu räumen,
If I fail to kill you,	darf ich doch nicht rasten:
how can I be sure of my treasure,	Wie käm' ich sonst anders zur Beute,
since Alberich covets it too?	da Alberich auch nach ihr lugt?

(He pours the brew into the drinking-horn and offers it to Siegfried with pressing gestures.) [51c]

Now, my Wälsung! [19]	Nun, mein Wälsung,
Wolf's son you!	Wolfssohn du!
Drink and choke to death! [17]	Sauf und würg dich zu Tod:
You'll never drink again!	nie tust du mehr 'nen Schluck!

(Siegfried raises his sword and seized by violent loathing, strikes Mime, who immediately falls dead.) [46]

SIEGFRIED

Taste then my sword,	Schmeck du mein Schwert,
horrible babbler!	ekliger Schwätzer!

(Alberich's mocking laughter is heard from the rocks. [17] *Siegfried quietly puts his sword back again, gazing at the fallen body.)* [17, 19]

Hatred's paid	Neides Zoll
by Notung:	zahlt Notung:
that's why I needed to forge it.	dazu durft' ich ihn schmieden.

(He grabs Mime's body, drags it to the cave, and throws it down inside.) [23, 17, 45]

In the cavern there,	In der Höhle hier
lie with the hoard!	lieg auf dem Hort!
You schemed so long [23]	Mit zäher List
and strove for that gold;	erzieltest du ihn:
so now take your joy in that treasure!	jetzt magst du des Wonnigen walten!
Let me place this guardian	Einen guten Wächter

there by your side,
so from all thieves you'll be safe.
(*With a great effort he drags the body of the dragon to the entrance of the cave, blocking it completely.*) [52]

You lie there too, [21]	Da lieg auch du,
mighty dragon!	dunkler Wurm!
The glittering gold [6]	Den gleissenden Hort
you now can share	hüte zugleich
with your foe who longed for its gleam;	mit dem beuterührigen Feind:
and so you both have found your rest!	so fandet beide ihr nun Ruh'!

(*He gazes thoughtfully down into the cave for a while, and then returns slowly downstage as if tired. It is noon. He wipes his hand across his forehead.*) [52, 17]

I'm warm now	Heiss ward mir
from my heavy task!	von der harten Last!
Fever seems	Brausend jagt
to fire my blood.	mein brünst'ges Blut;
This hand burns on my brow.	die Hand brennt mir am Haupt.
High stands the sun above me;	Hoch steht schon die Sonne:
his brilliant eye	aus lichtem Blau
blazes down	blickt ihr Aug'
from the blue and beats on my head.	auf den Scheitel steil mir herab.
Here it's cooler; [53a, b]	Linde Kühlung
I'll rest under the branches!	erkies ich unter der Linde!

(*He lies down under the lime-tree and again looks up into the branches.*) [48a]

You're back then, dearest woodbird,	Noch einmal, liebes Vöglein,
not flown away [48b]	da wir so lang
after the fight?	lästig gestört,
Let me hear again your singing!	lauscht' ich gerne deinem Sange:
On a branch I see you	auf dem Zweige seh ich
swaying and swinging;	wohlig dich wiegen;
chirping and chirruping	zwitschernd umschwirren
brothers and sisters	dich Brüder und Schwestern,
surround you with laughter and love!	umschweben dich lustig und lieb!
But I am quite alone,	Doch ich — bin so allein,
have no brothers nor sisters;	hab nicht Brüder noch Schwestern:
and my mother died,	meine Mutter schwand,
my father fell,	mein Vater fiel:
unknown to their son!	nie sah sie der Sohn!
One comrade was mine, [17, 19]	Mein einziger Gesell
a detestable dwarf.	war ein garstiger Zwerg;
Love was never known	Güte zwang
between us;	uns nie zu Liebe;
cunning and sly,	listige Schlingen
he wanted to catch me;	warf mir der Schlaue;
so at last I was forced to kill him!	nun musst' ich ihn gar erschlagen!

(*Sadly, he looks into the branches again.*)

Dear little woodbird,	Freundliches Vöglein,
can you be my guide?	dich frage ich nun:
Can you tell me [48b]	gönntest du mir
where I'll find a friend?	wohl ein gut Gesell?
You must know some way to help me.	Willst du mir das Rechte raten?
So often I've called	Ich lockte so oft
and yet no-one has come.	und erlost' es mir nie:
You, my woodbird,	Du, mein Trauter,
you might do better,	träfst es wohl besser,
for you've advised me so well.	so recht ja rietest du schon.
Now sing! I'm listening for your song.	Nun sing! Ich lausche dem Sang.

VOICE OF THE WOODBIRD

Hi! Siegfried is free [53]	Hei! Siegfried erschlug
from the evil dwarf!	nun den schlimmen Zwerg!
Next he must awake	Jetzt wüsst ich ihm noch
his glorious bride:	das herrlichste Weib:
high on a mountain she sleeps,	Auf hohem Felsen sie schläft,
guarded by threatening flames.	Feuer umbrennt ihren Saal:

107

Who goes through the fire,	Durchschritt' er die Brunst,
wakens the bride.	weckt' er die Braut,
Brünnhilde then shall be his!	Brünnhilde wäre dann sein!

SIEGFRIED

(leaps up impetuously from his sitting position.)

O joyful song!	O holder Sang!
Sweet, happy strain!	Süssester Hauch!
Your glorious words	Wie brennt sein Sinn
strike fire in my breast;	mir sehrend die Brust!
like flames they burn me,	Wie zückt er heftig
kindle my heart!	zündend mein Herz!
What new thought inspires	Was jagt mir so jach
my heart and senses?	durch Herz und Sinne?
Tell me, my dear, sweet friend!	Sag es mir, süsser Freund!

VOICE OF THE WOODBIRD

Gaily in grief,	[53]	Lustig im Leid
I sing of love;		sing ich von Liebe;
joyful in woe,		wonnig aus Weh
I weave my song;		web ich mein Lied:
and lovers can tell what it means.		nur Sehnende kennen den Sinn!

SIEGFRIED

Joy fills me;		Fort jagt mich's
shouting with gladness,		jauchzend von hinnen,
forth I shall go to that rock!	[14]	fort aus dem Wald auf den Fels!
But one thing more tell me,		Noch einmal sage mir,
dearest woodbird:		holder Sänger:
say, can I pass through the fire?		werd ich das Feuer durchbrechen?
Can I awaken the bride?	[39]	Kann ich erwecken die Braut?

(Siegfried listens again.) [43]

VOICE OF THE WOODBIRD

Who wakens the maid,	[53]	Die Braut gewinnt,
Brünnhilde the bride,		Brünnhilde erweckt
no coward can be:		ein Feiger nie:
one unacquainted with fear!		nur wer das Fürchten nicht kennt!

SIEGFRIED

(laughs with delight.)

A foolish boy,	[53]	Der dumme Knab',
unacquainted with fear,		der das Fürchten nicht kennt,
dear woodbird, why, that's me!		mein Vöglein, der bin ja ich!
Today in vain		Noch heute gab ich
I attempted to learn —		vergebens mir Müh',
I hoped that the dragon could teach me.		das Fürchten von Fafner zu lernen:
Now joy fills my heart,		nun brenn ich vor Lust,
since from Brünnhild I'll learn it!		es von Brünnhild zu wissen!
What way must I take to the rock?		Wie find ich zum Felsen den Weg?

(The bird flutters out, circles over Siegfried, and then flies off hesitantly.)

Fluttering overhead, you guide me;	So wird mir der Weg gewiesen:
and where you flutter,	wohin du flatterst,
there I shall go!	folg ich dir nach!

(He pursues the bird, which for a while teasingly leads him in different directions: then it takes a definite course upstage and flies away. Siegfried follows. The curtain falls.) [53]

Act Three

A wild place at the foot of a rocky mountain which rises steeply at the left towards the back. Night; storm, lightning and violent thunder; the latter ceases after a while but the lightning continues to flash through the clouds. [24, 34, 36b, 9a, 25, 49a, 5x, 42, 38]

Scene One. *The Wanderer strides resolutely to a huge and cavernous opening in a rock downstage and stands there, leaning on his spear, while he calls into the mouth of the cave.*

WANDERER

Waken, Wala!		Wache, Wala!
Wala! Awake!	[55]	Wala, erwach!
From lasting sleep		Aus langem Schlaf
rise and appear at my call.		weck ich dich Schlummernde auf.
I call you again:		Ich rufe dich auf:
Arise! Arise!		Herauf! Herauf!
From earth's hidden caves,		Aus nebliger Gruft,
imprisoned in darkness, arise!		aus nächtigem Grunde herauf!
Erda! Erda!	[24]	Erda! Erda!
Woman all-wise!		Ewiges Weib!
From silence and darkness		Aus heimischer Tiefe
rise to the world!		tauche zur Höh'!
With spells I rouse you;		Dein Wecklied sing ich,
rise up and answer.		dass du erwachest;
Your slumbering wisdom		aus sinnendem Schlafe
I would awake.		weck ich dich auf.
All-knowing one!	[25]	Allwissende!
Wisdom's guardian!		Urweltweise!
Erda! Erda!		Erda! Erda!
Woman all-wise!	[55]	Ewiges Weib!
Waken, awaken,		Wache, erwache,
O Wala! Awaken!	[9a]	du Wala! Erwache!

(*The cave begins to glow with a bluish light, in which Erda is seen rising very slowly from the depths. She appears to be covered with hoar-frost: her hair and garments throw off a glimmering brightness.*) [38, 42]

ERDA

Strong is your call;	Stark ruft das Lied;
mighty spells have roused me.	kräftig reizt der Zauber.
From wisdom's dreams,	Ich bin erwacht
I rise at your call.	aus wissendem Schlaf.
Who drives my slumber hence?	Wer scheucht den Schlummer mir?

WANDERER

The Wanderer wakes you;	[24, 25]	Der Weckrufer bin ich
I need your wisdom;		und Weisen üb ich,
my spells have called you		dass weithin wache,
from caverns far below.		was fester Schlaf verschliesst.
On earth I have wandered,	[49a]	Die Welt durchzog ich,
far I have roamed;		wanderte viel,
I searched for wisdom,		Kunde zu werben,
strove day and night to achieve it.		urweisen Rat zu gewinnen.
No one on earth		Kundiger gibt es
is wiser than you;		keine als dich;
you know what's hid		bekannt ist dir,
in the caves of night,		was die Tiefe birgt,
what hill and dale,		was Berg und Tal,
air and water do hold.		Luft und Wasser durchwebt.
Where life is found,		Wo Wesen sind,
Erda is stirring;		wehet dein Atem;
where brains are brooding,		wo Hirne sinnen,
you stir their thoughts.		haftet dein Sinn:
All things, all things,		alles, sagt man,

all you must know.
Seeking wisdom and counsel,
I have waked you from sleep!

sei dir bekannt.
[55] Dass ich nun Kunde gewänne,
weck ich dich aus dem Schlaf!

[9a]

ERDA

My sleep is dreaming;
my dreaming, brooding.
My brooding brings all my wisdom.
But while I sleep
the Norns are waking,
and winding their cord,
and weaving all that I know:
the Norns can give your answer.

[42] Mein Schlaf ist Träumen,
mein Träumen Sinnen,
mein Sinnen Walten des Wissens.
[1b] Doch wenn ich schlafe,
wachen Nornen:
sie weben das Seil
und spinnen fromm, was ich weiss.
Was fragst du nicht die Nornen?

WANDERER

They weave for the world,
spin what you tell them,
but cannot change that world with their
weaving.
But you are wiser;
you can advise me
if the swift-turning wheel can be stopped.

[6] Im Zwange der Welt
weben die Nornen:
[25] sie können nichts wenden noch wandeln.

Doch deiner Weisheit
[55] dank' ich den Rat wohl,
wie zu hemmen ein rollendes Rad?

ERDA

Deeds of men
have beclouded all my thoughts;
my wisdom itself
once felt a conqueror's force.
A brave daughter
I bore to Wotan;
at his command
she chose heroes for Walhall.
She is valiant
and wise as well:
so why wake me?
You will learn your answer
from Erda's and Wotan's child.

[6] Männertaten
umdämmern mir den Mut:
mich Wissende selbst
[25] bezwang ein Waltender einst.
[8] Ein Wunschmädchen
gebar ich Wotan;
der Helden Wal
hiess für sich er sie küren.
[34, 43] Kühn ist sie
und weise auch:
Was weckst du mich
[38] und frägst um Kunde
nicht Erdas und Wotans Kind?

[8, 9a]

WANDERER

The Valkyrie daughter,
Brünnhild the maid.
She disobeyed the lord of the tempest
when he'd controlled the storm in his
breast:
when his son was in need
he longed to help him,
yet he renounced him
and doomed him to death.
She knew his will,
yet she defied him
and dared to break his commandment —
Brünnhild herself in her pride.
Wotan then
dealt with the maid;
and he closed her eyelids in sleep;
on that rock asleep she lies.
That holy maid
can be wakened alone,
roused by some man who makes her his
bride.
What can I learn from the maid?

Die Walküre meinst du,
[41] Brünnhild, die Maid?
Sie trotzte dem Stürmebezwinger:
wo er am stärksten selbst sich bezwang.

Was den Lenker der Schlacht
zu tun verlangte,
doch dem er wehrte
zuwider sich selbst,
allzu vertraut
wagte die Trotzige
[34] das für sich zu vollbringen,
Brünnhild in brennender Schlacht.
[37] Streitvater
strafte die Maid;
in ihr Auge drückte er Schlaf;
auf dem Felsen schläft sie fest.
Erwachen wird
die Weihliche nur,
[7b] um einen Mann zu minnen als Weib.

[38, 44] Frommten mir Fragen an sie?

ERDA

(is lost in dreams; she begins again after a long silence.)

My waking	Wirr wird mir,
leaves me confused:	seit ich erwacht:
wild and strange	wild und kraus
seems the world. [42]	kreist die Welt!
The Valkyrie,	Die Walküre,
the Wala's child,	der Wala Kind,
lay in fetters of sleep,	büsst' in Banden des Schlafs,
while her all-knowing mother slept? [38]	als die wissende Mutter schlief?
How can pride's teacher [41]	Der den Trotz lehrte,
punish pride?	straft den Trotz?
He who urged the doing,	Der die Tat entzündet,
punish the deed?	zürnt um die Tat?
He who rules by right,	Der die Rechte wahrt,
to whom truth is sacred,	der die Eide hütet,
scorn what is right,	wehret dem Recht,
rule by falsehood?	herrscht durch Meineid?
I'll return to the dark, [38]	Lass mich wieder hinab?
seal in slumber my wisdom!	Schlaf verschliesse mein Wissen!

WANDERER

O mother, you may not leave: [55]	Dich, Mutter, lass ich nicht ziehn,
You are bound by my mighty power.	da des Zaubers mächtig ich bin.
All-wise one,	Urwissend
you drove a thorn	stachest du einst
of cares and sorrow	der Sorge Stachel
in Wotan's fearless heart:	in Wotans wagendes Herz:
with fear of ruin, [24]	mit Furcht vor schmachvoll
shameful downfall [25]	feindlichem Ende
you filled his spirit,	füllt' ihm dein Wissen,
by words of warning and doom.	dass Bangen band seinen Mut.
If you are the world's [49a]	Bist du der Welt
wisest of women,	weisestes Weib,
say to me now:	sage mir nun:
how a god can master his care? [9a]	wie besiegt die Sorge der Gott?

ERDA

You are not	Du bist — nicht,
what you declare! [6]	was du dich nennst!
Why come here, stubborn and wild one,	Was kamst du, störrischer Wilder,
to trouble the Wala's sleep? [25]	zu stören der Wala Schlaf?

WANDERER

You are not [55]	Du bist — nicht,
what you have dreamed.	was du dich wähnst!
Wisdom of ages [25]	Urmütter-Weisheit
finds its ending.	geht zu Ende:
Your wisdom grows weak	dein Wissen verweht
before my wishes.	vor meinem Willen.
Know you what Wotan wills? [5x]	Weisst du, was Wotan will?

(long silence)

You unwise one, [24]	Dir Unweisen
learn what I will,	ruf ich ins Ohr,
then carefree you may sleep in peace! [25]	dass sorglos ewig du nun schläfst!
That the gods may die soon	Um der Götter Ende
gives me no anguish;	grämt mich die Angst nicht,
I have willed that end!	seit mein Wunsch es will!
What in an hour of fiercest anguish	Was in des Zwiespalts wildem Schmerze
despairing once I resolved	verzweifelnd einst ich beschloss,
freely and gladly	froh und freudig
I shall now bring to pass. [56]	führe frei ich nun aus.
Once I declared in my loathing	Weiht' ich in wütendem Ekel
the Niblung might claim all the world;	des Niblungen Neid schon die Welt,
today to the Wälsung [39]	dem herrlichsten Wälsung

I have bequeathed my realm.　　　　[8, 46]　weis ich mein Erbe nun an.
　　One who has never known me,　　　　　　　Der von mir erkoren,
　　though chosen by me,　　　　　　　　　　doch nie mich gekannt,
　　a youth of dauntless daring,　　　　　　　ein kühnester Knabe,
　　unhelped by Wotan,　　　　　　　　　　　bar meines Rates,
has gained the Nibelung's ring.　　　[6, 27]　errang des Niblungen Ring.
　　Free from hate,　　　　　　　　　　　　Liebesfroh,
　　joyful and loving,　　　　　　　　　　　ledig des Neides,
　　that youth is not harmed　　　　　　　　erlahmt an dem Edlen
　　by Alberich's curse,　　　　　　　[39]　Alberichs Fluch;
for he knows naught of fear.　　　　　　　　denn fremd bleibt ihm die Furcht.
　　She whom you once bore,　　　　　[30]　Die du mir gebarst,
　　Brünnhild　　　　　　　　　　　　　　Brünnhild,
wakes to that hero's kiss.　　　　　　[56]　weckt sich hold der Held:
　　Then your wisdom's　　　　　　　　　　wachend wirkt
　　child will achieve　　　　　　　　　　　dein wissendes Kind
that deed that will free our world.　　　　　erlösende Weltentat.
　　So back to your dreams;　　　　　　　　Drum schlafe nun du,
　　dream on in darkness;　　　　　　[42]　schliesse dein Auge;
dream of the gods' destruction.　　　　　　träumend erschau mein Ende!
　　Whatever may happen,　　　　　　　　　Was jene auch wirken,
　　the god will gladly　　　　　　　[56]　dem ewig Jungen
yield his rule to the young!　　　　　　　　weicht in Wonne der Gott.
　　Return then, Erda!　　　　　　　[55]　Hinab denn, Erda!
　　Mother of dread!　　　　　　　　　　　Urmütterfurcht!
　　World-sorrow!　　　　　　　　　　　　Ursorge!
　　Return! Return　　　　　　　　　　　　Hinab! Hinab
　　to endless sleep!　　　　　　　　[42]　zu ew'gem Schlaf!

Erda has already closed her eyes and gradually begun to descend. She now disappears entirely; the cavernous opening too has become completely dark. The moon lights the scene. The storm has ceased.

Scene Two. *The Wanderer has walked up to the cave: he leans back against the rock, facing the stage.*

WANDERER

I see that Siegfried is near.　　　　　　　　Dort seh ich Siegfried nahn.
(He remains in his position by the cave. Siegfried's woodbird flutters downstage, then suddenly stops, flutters hither and thither as if alarmed, and disappears hastily at the back.) [53]

SIEGFRIED
(enters downstage right, and pauses.)

My woodbird flew from my sight.　　　　　Mein Vöglein schwebte mir fort!
　　With fluttering wings,　　　　　[48a]　Mit flatterndem Flug
　　and sweetest songs,　　　　　　　　　und süssem Sang
gaily he showed me my path;　　　　　　　wies es mich wonnig des Wegs:
but now he's fluttered away!　　　　　[54]　nun schwand es fern mir davon!
　　So I'll discover　　　　　　　　　　　Am besten find ich mir
　　the rock for myself.　　　　　　　　　selbst nun den Berg.
The path my bird pointed out,　　　　　　Wohin mein Führer mich wies,
that path I must pursue.　　　　　　[53d]dahin wandr' ich jetzt fort.
(He goes upstage.)

WANDERER

　　Young man, hear me;　　　　　　　　Wohin, Knabe,
　　where are you going?　　　　　　　　heisst dich dein Weg?

SIEGFRIED
(pauses and turns round.)

　　Who speaks to me?　　　　　　　[53]　Da redet's ja;
　　Can he show me my path?　　　　　　　wohl rät das mir den Weg.
(He approaches the Wanderer.)
　　I must find a mountain,　　　　　[4]　Einen Felsen such ich,
by blazing fire it's surrounded:　　　　[53]　von Feuer ist der umwabert:
　　there sleeps a maid:　　　　　　　　　Dort schläft ein Weib,
　　I must waken her!　　　　　　　　　　das ich wecken will.

Who told you then
to seek this mountain?
Who said this maid would be found there?

Wer sagt' es dir,
den Fels zu suchen?
Wer, nach der Frau dich zu sehnen?

SIEGFRIED

I heard a lovely
woodbird sing:
it told me of the mountain.

Mich wies ein singend
Waldvöglein,
das gab mir gute Kunde.

WANDERER

A woodbird chirps as it pleases;
but men don't understand;
so how did you know
what it was singing?

Ein Vöglein schwatzt wohl manches;
kein Mensch doch kann's verstehn.
Wie mochtest du Sinn
dem Sang entnehmen?

SIEGFRIED

I tasted a drop
of a dragon's blood
who fell at Neidhöhl before me;
and when I'd tasted
that fiery blood,
then the birdsong I heard clear as speech.

[52] Das wirkte das Blut
eines wilden Wurms,
der mir vor Neidhöhl erblasste.
Kaum netzt' es zündend
die Zunge mir,
da verstand ich der Vöglein Gestimm'.

WANDERER

To fight so fierce a foe,
who urged you on —
if you have really killed the dragon?

Erschlugst den Riesen du,
wer reizte dich,
den starken Wurm zu bestehn?

SIEGFRIED

My guide was Mime,
an evil dwarf,
when fear he wanted to teach me;
and then the dragon
urged me himself,
dared me to use my sword,
when he opened threatening jaws.

Mich führte Mime,
ein falscher Zwerg;
das Fürchten wollt' er mich lehren.
[46] Zum Schwertstreich aber,
der ihn erschlug,
[52] reizte der Wurm mich selbst,
seinen Rachen riss er mir auf.

WANDERER

Who forged your sword
so sharp and true,
that it slew so fierce a foe?

Wer schuf das Schwert
so scharf und hart,
dass der stärkste Feind ihm fiel?

SIEGFRIED

I forged it myself,
when the smith was beaten:
swordless else I should be.

[44] Das schweisst' ich mir selbst,
[17] da's der Schmied nicht konnte:
schwertlos noch wär' ich wohl sonst.

WANDERER

But who made
the mighty fragments.
from which the sword could then be
forged?

Doch, wer schuf
die starken Stücken,
daraus das Schwert du dir geschweisst?

SIEGFRIED

Ha! How can I tell?
I only knew
that the broken sword was useless,
till I had forged it myself.

Was weiss ich davon?
Ich weiss allein,
dass die Stücken mir nichts nützten,
schuf ich das Schwert mir nicht neu.

WANDERER
(*breaks into a happy, good-humoured laugh.*)

That's certainly true!   Das — mein ich wohl auch!
(*He looks at Siegfried with approval.*) [31]

SIEGFRIED
(surprised)

You're laughing at me	Was lachst du mich aus?
with your questions!	Alter Frager!
Mock me no more,	Hör einmal auf:
keeping me here with your chatter.	lass mich nicht länger hier schwatzen!
Old man, if you	[31] Kannst du den Weg
can help me, then do so:	mir weisen, so rede:
and if you can't,	vermagst du's nicht,
then hold your tongue!	so halte dein Maul!

WANDERER

Young man, be patient!	Geduld, du Knabe!
If I seem old,	Dünk ich dich alt,
then you should honour the aged.	so sollst du Achtung mir bieten.

SIEGFRIED

Honour the aged!	Das wär' nicht übel!
When all my life	Solang ich lebe,
there stood in my path	stand mir ein Alter
an aged fellow;	stets im Wege;
now I have swept him away.	den hab ich nun fortgefegt.
If you stay longer,	[47] Stemmst du dort länger
trying to obstruct me,	steif dich mir entgegen —
have a care, old one,	sieh dich vor, sag ich,
or else, like Mime you'll fare!	dass du wie Mime nicht fährst!

(He goes closer to the Wanderer.) [53]

How strange you look!	Wie siehst du denn aus?
Why do you wear	Was hast du gar
such a great big hat?	für'nen grossen Hut?
Why have you pulled it down over your [31]	Warum hängt er dir so ins Gesicht?
face?	

WANDERER
(still without changing his position) [49a, 34]

That's how the Wanderer wears it,	Das ist so des Wand'rers Weise,
when against the wind he must go!	[8] wenn dem Wind entgegen er geht.

SIEGFRIED
(observes him more closely)

But an eye underneath it you're lacking?	Doch darunter fehlt dir ein Auge:
No doubt some stranger	Das schlug dir einer
once struck it out	gewiss schon aus,
when you decided	dem du zu trotzig
to bar his way?	den Weg vertratst?
Out of my way,	Mach dich jetzt fort,
or else you may lose	sonst könntest du leicht
the other eye that is left you.	das andere auch noch verlieren.

WANDERER

I see, my son,	[8] Ich seh, mein Sohn,
one thing you know —	wo du nichts weisst,
to get your way as you want it.	da weisst du dir leicht zu helfen.
Yet be careful,	Mit dem Auge,
for with eyes quite as blind	das als andres mir fehlt,
as that eye I've lost, you are gazing	erblickst du selber das eine,
on the eye that is left me for sight.	das mir zum Sehen verblieb.

SIEGFRIED
(who has listened thoughtfully, now involuntarily bursts out laughing.)

At least you're good for a laugh, then!	Zum Lachen bist du mir lustig!
But hear, I'm getting impatient;	Doch hör, nun schwatz ich nicht länger:
at once, show me my path,	geschwind, zeig mir den Weg,
then your own way find for yourself.	deines Weges ziehe dann du;
What use	zu nichts andrem

114

is a foolish old man?
So speak, or I'll push you aside!

acht ich dich nütz:
drum sprich, sonst spreng ich dich fort!

WANDERER
(*softly*) [36a]

Child, if you knew
who I am,
you'd then spare me your scorn!
Sad from one so dear
sounds such scornful defiance.
Dear to my heart
is your glorious race —
though I was harsh
and they shrank from my rage.
You, whom I love so,
youthful hero!
do not waken that rage;
it would ruin both you and me!

Kenntest du mich,
kühner Spross,
den Schimpf spartest du mir!
Dir so vertraut,
[31]   trifft mich schmerzlich dein Dräuen.
Liebt' ich von je
deine lichte Art,
[36a]   Grauen auch zeugt' ihr
mein zürnender Grimm.
Dem ich so hold bin,
Allzuhehrer,
heut nicht wecke mir Neid:
er vernichtete dich und mich!

SIEGFRIED

Still no reply,
stubborn old fool!
Out of my way then,
for that path, I know,
leads to the slumbering maid
I learnt from the woodbird
who now has fluttered away.

Bleibst du mir stumm,
störrischer Wicht?
Weich von der Stelle,
denn dorthin, ich weiss,
[30]   führt es zur schlafenden Frau.
[53]   So wies es mein Vöglein,
das hier erst flüchtig entfloh.

(*It quickly becomes quite dark again.*)

WANDERER
(*breaking out in anger, imperiously*)

It left you to save its life!
The ravens' ruler
it knew was here.
Ill fate follow its flight!
The path that it showed you
you shall not tread!

[5x]   Es floh dir zu seinem Heil!
Den Herrn der Raben
erriet es hier:
[9a]   weh ihm, holen sie's ein!
[39]   Den Weg, den es zeigte,
sollst du nicht ziehn!

SIEGFRIED
(*steps back astonished, but defiant.*) [36a]

Ho! Ho! So you'd stop me!
Who are you then
to say I can't go on?

Hoho, du Verbieter!
Wer bist du denn,
dass du mir wehren willst?

WANDERER

I am the rock's defender!
And mine the spell
that enfolds the slumbering maid.
He who can wake her,
he who can win her,
makes me powerless for ever!
A sea of flame
now circles the maid,
burning and blazing
protects the rock.
He who seeks the bride
must brave that barrier of flame.

Fürchte des Felsens Hüter!
Verschlossen hält!
meine Macht die schlafende Maid:
wer sie erweckte,
wer sie gewänne,
[13a]   machtlos macht' er mich ewig!
Ein Feuermeer
unflutet die Frau,
glühende Lohe
umleckt den Fels:
wer die Braut begehrt,
dem brennt entgegen die Brunst.

(*He points with his spear to the rocky heights.*)

Look, on the heights!
Can you see that light?
The splendour grows,
the flames leap high;
fire clouds are rolling,
lightning is flashing,
raging and roaring
and coming this way.

[34, 14]   Blick nach der Höh'!
Erlugst du das Licht?
Es wächst der Schein,
es schwillt die Glut;
sengende Wolken,
[42]   wabernde Lohe
wälzen sich brennend
und prasselnd herab:

115

A light-flood   ein Lichtmeer
now shines round your head.   umleuchtet dein Haupt:
(*On the summit, a flickering fire becomes more and more clearly visible.*)
And soon that fire   Bald frisst und sehrt dich
will seize and destroy you.   zündendes Feuer.
Stand back, then, foolhardy boy!   Zurück denn, rasendes Kind!

SIEGFRIED

Stand back, old boaster, yourself!   [39] Zurück, du Prahler, mit dir!
There, where the flames are burning,   [4, 53] Dort, wo die Brünste brannen,
to Brünnhilde now I shall go!   [43] zu Brünnhilde muss ich dahin!
(*He advances; the Wanderer bars his way.*)

WANDERER

If you've no fear of the fire,   Fürchtest das Feuer du nicht,
(*stretching out his spear*)
the shaft of my spear bars your way!   [9a, 36a] sperre mein Speer dir den Weg!
I grasp in my hand   Noch hält meine Hand
that mighty shaft;   der Herrschaft Haft:
the sword that you bear   das Schwert, das du schwingst,
was broken by this shaft;   zerschlug einst dieser Schaft:
and once again   noch einmal denn
I'll break it on this my spear!   zerspring es am ew'gen Speer!
(*He stretches out his spear.*)

SIEGFRIED
(*drawing his sword*)

Then my father's foe   [31] Meines Vaters Feind!
faces me here?   Find ich dich hier?
Glorious vengeance   Herrlich zur Rache
I've found at last!   geriet mir das!
Stretch out your spear: [27] Schwing deinen Speer:
and see it break on my sword!   in Stücken spalt' ihn mein Schwert!
(*Siegfried with one blow strikes the Wanderer's spear in two: a streak of lightning flashes from it towards the summit, where the flames, glowing dully before, now break out more and more brightly. The blow is accompanied by a violent clap of thunder that quickly dies away. The fragments of the spear fall at the Wanderer's feet. He quickly picks them up.*) [9a]

WANDERER
(*falling back*)

Pass on! I cannot prevent you!   [24, 25] Zieh hin! Ich kann dich nicht halten!
(*He suddenly disappears in complete darkness.*)

SIEGFRIED

With his spear in splinters,   [31] Mit zerfochtner Waffe
He has escaped me!   [39] floh mir der Feige?
(*Siegfried's attention is caught by the growing brightness of the fire-clouds as they roll down the mountain.*)
Ha! Flame of delight!   [4, 53] Ha! Wonnige Glut!
Glorious blaze!   Leuchtender Glanz!
Shining, my pathway   Strahlend nun offen
opens before me.   steht mir die Strasse.
In fire I shall find her!   Im Feuer mich baden!
Through fire I shall make her mine!   Im Feuer zu finden die Braut!
Hoho! Hahi!   Hoho! Hahei!
My comrade shall wake to my call!   Jetzt lock ich ein liebes Gesell!
(*Siegfried raises his horn to his lips and, playing his call, plunges into the sea of fire, which has swept down from the heights and is spreading across the forestage. Siegfried seems to be climbing up to the peak; soon he is no longer visible. The flames reach their brightest, and then begin to fade, gradually dissolving into a finer and finer mist, lit as if by the red of the dawn.*)
[45, 14, 39, 4, 53, 13a, 42, 43]

Scene Three. *The clouds, which have become increasingly fine dissolve into a veil of rosy mist, which now divides. The upper part drifts away altogether, revealing at last only the bright blue sky of daylight, while on the edge of the rocky height, which now becomes visible — exactly the same scene as in Act Three of 'The Valkyrie' — there hangs a veil of reddish morning mist, suggesting the magic fire that still rages below. The arrangement of the scene is precisely as at the end of 'The Valkyrie': downstage, under the wide-spreading fir tree, lies Brünnhilde in full shining armour, her helmet on her head, and her long shield covering her. She is in a deep sleep.* [43, 38, 11a]

SIEGFRIED

(reaches the rocky summit of the cliff from the back. At first only the upper part of his body is visible. He looks around for a while in astonishment.)

Here, in the sunlight,	Selige Öde
a haven of calm!	auf sonniger Höh!

(He climbs right to the top and, standing on a rock at the edge of the precipice at the back, surveys the scene with wonder. He looks into the wood at the side and takes a step or two towards it.) [53a, 10, 11a]

What lies there sleeping		Was ruht dort schlummernd
in the shade of the pines?		im schattigen Tann?
A horse there,	[34]	Ein Ross ist's,
resting in deepest sleep!		rastend in tiefem Schlaf!

(Coming forward slowly, he pauses in astonishment as he sees Brünnhilde's form some distance away.) [43a]

What flashes in the sunlight?	Was strahlt mir dort entgegen?
What glittering steel is there?	Welch glänzendes Stahlgeschmeid?
Is it the fire	Blendet mir noch
still dazzling my eyes?	die Lohe den Blick?

(He comes closer)

Shining armour?	Helle Waffen!
Let me approach!	Heb ich sie auf?

(He raises the shield and sees Brünnhilde's form, though her face is still largely concealed by the helmet.)

Ha! in armour, a man.		Ha, in Waffen ein Mann!
My heart most strangely is stirred!		Wie mahnt mich wonnig sein Bild!
His noble head		Das hehre Haupt
pressed by the helm?		drückt wohl der Helm?
Shall I loose it,	[10]	Leichter würd' ihm,
easing his ears?		löst' ich den Schmuck.

(He carefully loosens the helmet and removes it from the sleeper; long curling hair falls down. Siegfried starts.)

Ah! How fair!	Ach! Wie schön!

(He cannot take his eyes from her.)

Shimmering clouds	Schimmernde Wolken
encircle in splendour	säumen in Wellen
a holy, heavenly sea;	den hellen Himmelssee;
glorious sunlight	leuchtender Sonne
streams from his face,	lachendes Bild
shines through the clouds all around!	strahlt durch das Wogengewölk!

(He bends lower towards the sleeper.)

The weight of the armour	Von schwellendem Atem
bears on his breast!	schwingt sich die Brust!
Shall I unfasten the breastplate?	Brech ich die engende Brünne?

(Carefully, he tries to loosen the breastplate.) [34]

Come, my sword!		Komm, mein Schwert,
Cut through the metal!	[27]	schneide das Eisen!

(He draws his sword and gently and carefully cuts through the rings of mail on both sides of the armour. Then he lifts off the breastplate and the greaves; Brünnhilde lies before him in soft woman's drapery. [7b] *He starts back in astonishment and alarm.)*

It's not a man!	Das ist kein Mann!

(He stares at the slumbering form with wildest emotion.) [10]

Blazing enchantments	Brennender Zauber
burn in my breast;	zückt mir ins Herz;
fiery spells	feurige Angst
dazzle and blind me;	fasst meine Augen:
my heart grows feeble and faint!	mir schwankt und schwindelt der Sinn!

117

On whom shall I call?	[31]	Wen ruf ich zum Heil,
Ah, who can help me?		dass er mir helfe?
Mother! Mother!		Mutter, Mutter!
Remember me!		Gedenke mein!

(He falls, as if fainting, on Brünnhilde's breast. A long silence. He rises with a sigh.) [31]

How waken the maid,		Wie weck ich die Maid,
and see her eyes gently open?		dass sie ihr Auge mir öffne?
Her eyes gently open?		Das Auge mir öffne?
Will they not dazzle and blind?		Blende mich auch noch der Blick?
How can I dare		Wagt' es mein Trotz?
to gaze on their light?		Ertrüg' ich das Licht?
Beneath my feet	[31]	Mir schwebt und schwankt
the ground seems to sway!		und schwirrt es umher!
Anguish and yearning		Sehrendes Sehnen
conquer my courage;		zehrt meine Sinne;
on my heart, beating wildly,		am zagenden Herzen
trembles my hand!	[43]	zittert die Hand!
Am I a coward?		Wie ist mir Feigem?
Is this what fear is?		Ist dies das Fürchten?
Oh mother! Mother!	[31]	O Mutter, Mutter!
Your bold fearless child!		Dein mutiges Kind!
A woman lies here in sleep,	[43]	Im Schlafe liegt eine Frau:
and she now has taught me to fear!	[11a]	die hat ihn das Fürchten gelehrt!
How conquer my fear?		Wie end ich die Furcht?
How steel my heart?		Wie fass ich Mut?
If I am to awake myself,		Das ich selbst erwache,
first the maid must awaken.	[27]	muss die Maid ich erwecken!

(As he approaches the sleeper again he is again filled with tender emotion at the sight of her. He bends lower over her.)

Sweet and quivering,		Süss erbebt mir
her lovely mouth	[30a, 10]	ihr blühender Mund.
A gentle gladness		Wie mild erzitternd
charms fear from my heart!		mich Zagen er reizt!
Ah! How enchanting		Ach! Dieses Atems
her warm, fragrant breath!		wonnig warmes Gedüft!
Awaken! Awaken!		Erwache! Erwache!
Holiest maid!		Heiliges Weib!

(He gazes upon her.) [38]

She hears me not.	Sie hört mich nicht.

(slowly, with tense and urgent expression)

Then life I shall gather		So saug ich mir Leben
from lips filled with sweetness;		aus süssesten Lippen,
what though I die by this kiss!	[7b]	sollt' ich auch sterbend vergehn!

(He falls, as if dying, on the sleeping figure, and with closed eyes presses his lips on her mouth. Brünnhilde opens her eyes. Siegfried starts up and stands before her. Brünnhilde slowly rises to a sitting position. She raises her arms and salutes the heaven and earth with solemn gestures now that she sees them again.) [7b, 11a, 57]

BRÜNNHILDE

Hail, bright sunlight!		Heil dir, Sonne!
Hail, fair sky!		Heil dir, Licht!
Hail, O radiant day!		Heil dir, leuchtender Tag!
Long was my sleep;	[38]	Lang war mein Schlaf;
but now I wake:		ich bin erwacht.
Who is the man		Wer ist der Held,
wakes me to life?		der mich erweckt?

SIEGFRIED

(deeply moved by her look and her voice, stands as if rooted to the spot.)

I have braved the dangers	[39]	Durch das Feuer drang ich,
blazing round your rock;		das den Fels umbrann;
from your head I unclasped the helm;		ich erbrach dir den festen Helm:
Siegfried wakes you,		Siegfried bin ich,
brings you to life.		der dich erweckt.

(sitting straight up)

Wotan, hear me	Heil euch, Götter!
Hear me, world!	Heil dir, Welt!
Hear me, glorious nature!	Heil dir, prangende Erde!
My sleep is at an end;	Zu End' ist nun mein Schlaf;
awake I see	erwacht, seh ich:
Siegfried! Siegfried	Siegfried ist es,
has brought me to life!	der mich erweckt!

SIEGFRIED
(breaking out in ecstasy)

I bless my mother,	[59]	O Heil der Mutter,
giving me birth!		die mich gebar;
bless the earth		Heil der Erde,
that gave me my strength! —		die mich genährt!
now I behold your eyes,		Dass ich das Aug' erschaut,
bright stars that laugh on my joy!		das jetzt mir Seligem lacht!

BRÜNNHILDE
(with deep emotion)

I bless your mother,	[59]	O Heil der Mutter,
giving you birth!		die dich gebar!
bless the earth		Heil der Erde,
that gave you your strength!		die dich genährt!
Your eyes alone could behold me;		Nur dein Blick durfte mich schaun,
my heart to you alone wakes!		erwachen durft' ich nur dir.

(Each remains lost in radiant, rapt contemplation of the other.) [31, 39, 58]

O Siegfried! Siegfried!	[59]	O Siegfried! Siegfried!
Radiant hero!		Seliger Held!
Victorious conqueror,	[58, 39]	Du Wecker des Lebens,
conquering light!		siegendes Licht!
O learn from me, joy of the world,	[59]	O wüsstest du, Lust der Welt,
how I have always loved you!		wie ich dich je geliebt!
You were my gladness,		Du warst mein Sinnen,
my cares as well!		mein Sorgen du!
Your life I sheltered,		Dich Zarten nährt' ich,
in Sieglinde's womb;		noch eh du gezeugt;
before she had borne you,		noch eh du geboren,
I was your shield.		barg dich mein Schild:
So long I have loved, Siegfried!	[56]	so lang lieb ich dich, Siegfried!

SIEGFRIED
(softly and shyly)

My mother is alive, then?	[31]	So starb nicht meine Mutter?
Sleep enfolded her here?		Schlief die Minnige nur?

BRÜNNHILDE
(smiling, and stretching out her hand to him in friendship)

O innocent child!	[58]	Du wonniges Kind!
Nevermore you'll look on your mother.		Deine Mutter kehrt dir nicht wieder.
But we are one,		Du selbst bin ich,
if you can grant me your love.		wenn du mich Selige liebst.
What you would learn,	[38]	Was du nicht weisst,
learn it from me,		weiss ich für dich;
for wisdom fills my soul!	[56]	doch wissend bin ich
now that I love you!		nur — weil ich dich liebe!
O Siegfried! Siegfried!	[59]	O Siegfried! Siegfried!
conquering light!		Siegendes Licht!
I loved you always,	[58]	Dich liebt' ich immer;
for I divined		denn mir allein
the thought that Wotan had hidden,	[37]	erdünkte Wotans Gedanke.
guessed the secret thought		Der Gedanke, den ich nie
I dared not even whisper;		nennen durfte;
I did not shape it,		den ich nicht dachte,

rather I felt it;
and so I fought,
urged by that deed,
when I defied the god
who conceived it;
and then I suffered,
slept on this rock,
for that thought still secret,
that thought I felt!
Know what that thought was;
ah, you can guess it!
That thought was my love for you!

sondern nur fühlte;
für den ich focht,
[41] kämpfte und stritt;
für den ich trotzte
dem, der ihn dachte;
für den ich büsste,
Strafe mich band,
weil ich nicht ihn dachte
und nur empfand!
Denn der Gedanke —
[56] dürftest du's lösen! —
mir war er nur Liebe zu dir!

SIEGFRIED

Ah, glorious song,
enchanting to hear;
but yet the meaning is dark.
I can see your eyes
that shine so bright;
I can feel your warm
and fragrant breath;
I can hear your song
so clear and sweet:
but what your singing can mean,
how can I understand?
You sing of the past,
but how can I listen,
while I have you beside me,
see and feel only you?
In bonds of fear
I have been bound:
from you alone
could I learn how to fear.
Since you have bound me
in powerful fetters,
give me my freedom again!

[59] Wie Wunder tönt,
was wonnig du singst;
doch dunkel dünkt mich der Sinn.
Deines Auges Leuchten
seh ich licht;
deines Atems Wehen
fühl ich warm:
deiner Stimme Singen
hör ich süss:
doch was du singend mir sagst,
[38, 31] staunend versteh ich's nicht.
Nicht kann ich das Ferne
sinnig erfassen,
wenn alle Sinne
dich nur sehen und fühlen!
Mit banger Furcht
fesselst du mich:
du einz'ge hast
ihre Angst mich gelehrt.
Den du gebunden
in mächtigen Banden,
[7b] birg meinen Mut mir nicht mehr!

(He remains in profound agitation, throwing her looks of passionate yearning.) [27a]

BRÜNNHILDE
(gently turns her head aside and looks towards the wood.) [34, 30]

And there is Grane,
my sacred horse;
he grazes in gladness
where once he slept!
Like me, to Siegfried he wakes.

Dort seh ich Grane,
mein selig Ross:
wie weidet er munter,
der mit mir schlief!
Mit mir hat ihn Siegfried erweckt.

SIEGFRIED
(remaining in the same position) [59]

My eyes are grazing
on pastures more lovely;
with passionate thirst
my lips too are burning,
for they long to graze where my glance
does!

[58] Auf wonnigem Munde
weidet mein Auge:
in brünstigem Durst
doch brennen die Lippen,
[31] dass der Augen Weide sie labe!

BRÜNNHILDE
(points to her weapons, which she now perceives.) [27a]

And there is the shield
that sheltered heroes;
beside it the helmet
that hid my head.
They shield, they hide no more!

[30] Dort seh ich den Schild,
der Helden schirmte;
dort seh ich den Helm,
der das Haupt mir barg:
er schirmt, er birgt mich nicht mehr!

SIEGFRIED

Now a glorious maid
has wounded my heart;

Eine selige Maid
versehrte mein Herz;

wounds in my head
were struck by that maid:
I came with no shield or helm!

Wunden dem Haupte
schlug mir ein Weib:
Ich kam ohne Schild und Helm!

BRÜNNHILDE
(*with increasing sadness*)

And there is the steel
that guarded my breast.
A shining sword
cut it in two,
when the maid was stripped
of all her defence.
I have no defence, no shield;
quite unarmed, a sorrowing maid!

Ich sehe der Brünne
prangenden Stahl:
ein scharfes Schwert
schnitt sie entzwei;
von dem maidlichen Leibe
löst' es die Wehr;
ich bin ohne Schutz und Schirm,
ohne Trutz ein trauriges Weib!

SIEGFRIED

Through furious fire
I fared to your rock;
no breastplate, no armour
guarded my breast;
the flames have broken through
to my heart.
My blood's ablaze   [31]
and burns in my breast;
a passionate fire
within me is kindled;
that blaze which guarded
Brünnhilde's rock
now flames fiercely in my breast!
O maid, you started the fire!
You can extinguish the flame!

Durch brennendes Feuer
fuhr ich zu dir!
Nicht Brünne noch Panzer
barg meinen Leib:
Nun brach die Lohe
mir in die Brust.
Es braust mein Blut
in blühender Brunst;
ein sehrendes Feuer
ist mir entzündet:
Die Glut, die Brünnhilds
Felsen umbrann,
die brennt mir nun in der Brust!
O Weib, jetzt lösche den Brand!
Schweige die schäumende Glut!

(*He has embraced her passionately. She jumps up violently, repulses him with the utmost terror, and runs to the other side.*)

BRÜNNHILDE

No god dared to come near!
The heroes bowed
and knelt to the maiden:
holy came she from Walhall.   [8]
Sorrow! Sorrow!
Woe for my shame,
how keen my disgrace!   [39]
And he who wakes me
deals me the wound!
He has broken the breastplate and helm:
Brünnhilde am I no more!

Kein Gott nahte mir je!
Der Jungfrau neigten
scheu sich die Helden:
heilig schied sie aus Walhall!
Wehe! Wehe!
Wehe der Schmach,
der schmählichen Not!
Verwundet hat mich,
der mich erweckt!
Er erbrach mir Brünne und Helm:
Brünnhilde bin ich nicht mehr!

SIEGFRIED

You are still to me
that slumbering maid;
Brünnhilde's sleep
still binds her fast.
Awaken, you are my bride!

Noch bist du mir
die träumende Maid:
Brünnhildes Schlaf
brach ich noch nicht.
Erwache, sei mir ein Weib!

BRÜNNHILDE

My mind's in confusion,
my reason sways:
must all my wisdom fail me?

Mir schwirren die Sinne,
mein Wissen schweigt:
soll mir die Weisheit schwinden?

SIEGFRIED

You said   [56]
that all your wisdom came
by the light of your love for me.

Sangst du mir nicht,
dein Wissen sei
das Leuchten der Liebe zu mir?

BRÜNNHILDE
(staring in front of her)

Shadows of darkness	Trauriges Dunkel
close on me now.	trübt meinen Blick;
My eyes are blinded; [23]	mein Auge dämmert,
my sight grows dim.	das Licht verlischt:
Night falls around. [9b]	Nacht wird's um mich.
From darkness and gloom	Aus Nebel und Grau'n
wildly my fears	windet sich wütend
seem to seize on me. [5x]	ein Angstgewirr:
Dreadful horrors	Schrecken schreitet
arise in the dark!	und bäumt sich empor!

(She covers her eyes impulsively with her hands.) [30a]

SIEGFRIED
(gently removing her hands from her eyes)

Night enfolds	Nacht umfängt
those eyes you have hidden. [56]	gebundne Augen.
When I free them	Mit den Fesseln schwindet
all gloomy fears depart.	das finstre Grau'n.
Rise from the darkness, and see:	Tauch aus dem Dunkel und sieh:
bright as the sun, here shines the day!	sonnenhell leuchtet der Tag!

BRÜNNHILDE
(profoundly agitated)

Bright as the sun	Sonnenhell
shines but the day of my shame! [41]	leuchtet der Tag meiner Schmach! —
O Siegfried! Siegfried!	O Siegfried! Siegfried!
See my dismay!	Sieh meine Angst!

(Brünnhilde's expression reveals that a pleasing idea has come to her mind, and at this she turns again and looks tenderly at Siegfried.)

Ever loving,	Ewig war ich,
ever caring,	ewig bin ich,
caring with sweet	ewig in süss
warm, tender longing —	sehnender Wonne,
yes, always for your dear life!	doch ewig zu deinem Heil!
O Siegfried,	O Siegfried!
glorious hero!	Herrlicher!
Wealth of the world!	Hort der Welt!
Fair, laughing hero!	Leben der Erde!
Light of the earth!	Lachender Held!
Leave, ah, leave,	Lass, ach lass,
Leave me in peace!	lasse von mir!
Do not come near me	Nahe mir nicht
with passionate frenzy;	mit der wütenden Nähe!
do not pursue me	Zwinge mich nicht
with masterful might,	mit dem brechenden Zwang,
or else you'll destroy all our love!	zertrümmre die Traute dir nicht!
You've seen your face	Sahst du dein Bild
in the shining stream?	im klaren Bach?
And it delighted your eyes?	Hat es dich Frohen erfreut?
But when that water	Rührtest zur Woge
is stirred by a wave,	das Wasser du auf;
your smiling reflection	zerflösse die klare
breaks and is gone; [31]	Fläche des Bachs:
your face greets you no more	dein Bild sähst du nicht mehr,
when that shining stream is disturbed!	nur der Welle schankend Gewog'.
So disturb me no more;	So berühre mich nicht,
trouble me not!	trübe mich nicht!
Ever bright, [43]	Ewiglich
may you ever see	lachst du selig dann
in me your reflection,	aus mir dir entgegen,
brave and smiling and fair!	froh und heiter ein Held!
O Siegfried!	O Siegfried!
Laughing youth!	Lachender Spross!

Love yourself,
and leave me in peace;
destroy not this maid who is yours!

[38] Liebe dich
und lasse von mir:
[43] vernichte dein Eigen nicht!

SIEGFRIED

I love you:
did you but love me!
Mine I am no more:
were you but mine!
A sea of enchantment
flows around;
with all my senses
I see alone
those surging, glorious billows.
Though in the deep
I may not see my face,
burning, I long
for those cooling waters;
and now, as I am,
leap in the stream —
if only those waves
could engulf me forever,
my yearning would fade in the flood!
Awaken, Brünnhilde!
Waken, O maid!
Live in laughter,
sweetest delight!
Be mine! Be mine! Be mine!

Dich lieb ich:
o liebtest mich du!
Nicht hab ich mehr mich:
o hätte ich dich!
Ein herrlich Gewässer
wogt vor mir;
mit allen Sinnen
seh ich nur sie,
die wonnig wogende Welle.
Brach sie mein Bild,
so brenn ich nun selbst,
sengende Glut
in der Flut zu kühlen;
ich selbst, wie ich bin,
spring in den Bach:
[43] o dass seine Wogen
mich selig verschlängen,
[56] mein Sehnen schwänd' in der Flut!
[59] Erwache, Brünnhilde!
[58] Wache, du Maid!
Lache und lebe,
süsseste Lust!
Sei mein! Sei mein! Sei mein!

BRÜNNHILDE
(*seriously*)

O Siegfried! Yours
I have always been!

[59] O Siegfried! Dein
war ich von je!

SIEGFRIED
(*passionately*)

If you were mine,
be mine again!

Warst du's von je,
so sei es jetzt!

BRÜNNHILDE

Yours ever
I shall be!

[59] Dein werd ich
ewig sein!

SIEGFRIED

If you'll be mine,
be so today!
When in my arms
I hold you embraced,
feeling your heart
beating beside me,
joining our glances,
sharing one single breath,
eyes together,
mouth to mouth:
then I shall know
that Brünnhilde's truly mine!
End my doubts, let me now be sure
that now Brünnhilde's mine!

Was du sein wirst,
sei es mir heut!
[58] Fasst dich mein Arm,
umschling ich dich fest;
schlägt meine Brust
brünstig die deine;
zünden die Blicke,
[59] zehren die Atem sich;
Aug' in Auge,
Mund an Mund:
[56] dann bist du mir,
was bang du mir warst und wirst!
Dann brach sich die brennende Sorge,
ob jetzt Brünnhilde mein?

(*He embraces her.*)

BRÜNNHILDE

That I am yours?
Godly composure,
change into wildness;
virginal light,

[38, 31] Ob jetzt ich dein?
Göttliche Ruhe
rast mir in Wogen:
keuschestes Licht

flare into frenzy;
heavenly wisdom,
fly to the winds:
love, love alone
inspires all my heart!
That I am yours?
Siegfried! Siegfried!
Can you not see?
When my eyes blaze on you,   [21]
then are you not blind?
Does my arms' embrace
not set you on fire?
By the heat of my blood
in its passionate surge,
a fire is kindled —   [34]
can you not feel?
Tell me then, Siegfried,
do you not fear
this wild, passionate maid?

lodert in Gluten:
himmlisches Wissen
stürmt mir dahin,
Jauchzen der Liebe
jagt es davon!
Ob jetzt ich dein?
Siegfried! Siegfried!
Siehst du mich nicht?
Wie mein Blick dich verzehrt,
erblindest du nicht?
Wie mein Arm dich presst,
entbrennst du mir nicht?
Wie in Strömen mein Blut
entgegen dir stürmt,
das wilde Feuer,
fühlst du es nicht?
Fürchtest du, Siegfried,
fürchtest du nicht
[39] das wild wütende Weib?

(She embraces him passionately)

SIEGFRIED
(in joyous terror)

Ha!
In the fire our blood has kindled,
in the flames that glow from our glances,
in our burning, ardent enchantments,
I find again
my boldness of heart;
and what fear is, ah!
I have failed to learn;
what fear is, not even
you can teach!
My fear, I find,
has faded and gone like a dream!

Ha!
Wie des Blutes Ströme sich zünden,
wie der Blicke Strahlen sich zehren,
wie die Arme brünstig sich pressen,
kehrt mir zurück
mein kühner Mut,
und das Fürchten, ach!
das ich nie gelernt,
das Fürchten, das du
mich kaum gelehrt:
das Fürchten — mich dünkt,
[53] ich Dummer vergass es nun ganz!

(At these words he has involuntarily released Brünnhilde.)

BRÜNNHILDE
(laughing wildly in an outburst of extreme joy)

O radiant youth!   [35, 34]
O glorious hero!
My proudly fearless,
brave, noble boy!
Laughing I shall love you,   [58]
laughing, welcome my blindness,
laughing, let us be lost together,
in laughter die!
Farewell, Walhall's   [61]
bright glittering world!
Your glorious halls
now may fall to dust!
Farewell, proud, radiant,   [59]
godly race!
End in joy,
you eternal clan!
And rend, O Norns,
that rope you weave!
Gods may sink
to eternal night!
Twilight and darkness
seize all the clan!
I live by the light   [56]
of Siegfried's bright star!
He's mine forever,   [61]
he is my joy,
my wealth, my world,

O kindischer Held!
O herrlicher Knabe!
Du hehrster Taten
töriger Hort!
Lachend muss ich dich lieben,
lachend will ich erblinden,
lachend lass uns verderben,
lachend zugrunde gehn!
Fahr hin, Walhalls
leuchtende Welt!
Zerfall in Staub
deine stolze Burg!
Leb wohl, prangende
Götterpracht!
End in Wonne,
du ewig Geschlecht!
Zerreisst, ihr Nornen,
das Runenseil!
Götterdämm'rung,
dunkle herauf!
Nach der Vernichtung,
neble herein!
Mir strahlt zur Stunde
Siegfrieds Stern;
er ist mir ewig,
ist mir immer,
Erb' und Eigen,

my one and all!
Light of our loving,
laughter in death!

ein und all:
leuchtende Liebe,
[56, 58, 39] lachender Tod!

Laughing, you wake
in gladness to me!
Brünnhilde lives,
Brünnhilde laughs!
Blessed the day
that shines around us!
Blessed the sun
that lights our way!
Blessed the light
that dispels the night!
Blessed the world
where Brünnhilde lives!
She wakes, she lives,
she greets me with laughter.
All my light
is Brünnhilde's star!
She's mine forever,
she is my joy,
my wealth, my world,
my one and all!
Light of our loving,
laughter in death!

[61] Lachend erwachst
du Wonnige mir:
Brünnhilde lebt,
Brünnhilde lacht!
[59] Heil dem Tage,
der uns umleuchtet!
Heil der Sonne,
die uns bescheint!
Heil dem Licht,
das der Nacht enttaucht!
Heil der Welt,
der Brünnhilde lebt!
Sie wacht, sie lebt,
sie lacht mir entgegen.
Prangend strahlt
mir Brünnhildes Stern!
[61] Sie ist mir ewig,
ist mir immer,
Erb' und Eigen,
ein und all:
leuchtende Liebe,
[56, 58, 39] lachender Tod!

Brünnhilde throws herself into Siegfried's arms.

The curtain falls.

Gwyneth Jones as Brünnhilde and Jean Cox as Siegfried in Götz Friedrich's production at Covent Garden (photo: Donald Southern)

Selective discography by *Martin Hoyle*. For detailed analysis the enthusiast is referred to *Opera on Record*, ed. Alan Blyth (Hutchinson, 1979).

Conductor Opera House/ Orchestra	*Solti* Vienna PO	*Karajan* Berlin PO	*Furtwängler* Rome Radio	*Böhm* Bayreuth Festival	*Goodall* English National Opera	*Boulez* Bayreuth Festival
Siegfried	Wingassen	Thomas	Suthaus	Windgassen	Remedios	Jung
Brünnhilde	Nilsson	Dernesch	Mödl	Nilsson	Hunter	Jones
Wanderer	Hotter	Stewart	Frantz	Adam	Bailey	McIntyre
Mime	Stolze	Stolze	Patzak	Wohlfart	Dempsey	Zednik
Fafner	Böhme	Ridderbusch	Greindl	Böhme	Grant	Hubner
Alberich	Neidlinger	Kélémen	Pernerstorfer	Neidlinger	Hammond-Stroud	Becht
Erda	Höffgen	Dominguez	Klose	Soukoupová	Collins	Wenkel
Woodbird	Sutherland	Gayer	Streich	Koth	London	Sharp
Disc UK number	Decca SET242-6	DG 2740147	EMI RLS702	Philips 6747037	HMV SLS875	Ph 6769074
Tape UK number	K 3W31	3378049	–	–	TC-SLS875	–
Disc US number	London 1508	DG 2713003	–	–	–	Ph 6769072
Tape US number	1508	3378049	–	–	–	–

Bibliography

Wagner wrote *Eine Mitteilung an meine Freunde* (*A Communication to My Friends*, 1851) as an introduction for them to the form of *The Ring* and *Oper und Drama* (*Opera and Drama*, 1852) sets out these new theories of opera. Both essays are included in *The Complete Prose Works of Richard Wagner*, translated by W. Ashton Ellis (London, 1892) which, although neither accurate nor fluent, is the most widely available translation. Robert Hartford's chronicle of *Bayreuth: The Early Years ... as seen by the celebrated visitors and participants* (London, 1980), and the eye-witness account of the stage rehearsals for the first Bayreuth Festival in *Wagner Rehearsing the 'Ring'* by Heinrich Porges (trans. R. Jacobs, Cambridge, 1983) give vivid insights into the first cycles. The two massive volumes of *Cosima Wagner's Diaries* (I, 1869-77; II, 1878-83) make astonishing reading because of their frankness and comprehensiveness (ed. George-Dellin and Mack, trans. G. Skelton, London, 1978, 1980).

Apart from the works cited in notes by the contributors, there are numerous studies of different aspects Wagner's life and music. A new translation of his own autobiography, *My Life* (1870), by A. Gray, ed. M. Whittall, has been published by Cambridge (1983). New translations of other important essays are to be published shortly by Cambridge.

There are now a number of relatively modern studies in English devoted to *The Ring*. *Wagner's 'Ring': An Introduction* by Alan Blyth (London, 1980) contains simple musical synopses for the cycle in one compact volume. *I Saw the World End* by Deryck Cooke (Oxford, 1979) and *Wagner's 'Ring' and its Symbols* by Robert Donington (London, 1963) are brilliant and much more densely argued commentaries which have prompted in turn much discussion. Carl Dalhaus's perceptive *Musicdramas of Richard Wagner* (trans. M. Whittall, Cambridge, 1980) includes chapters on the cycle, and *The Wagner Companion* (ed. Peter Burbidge and Richard Sutton, London, 1979) includes several essays of especial interest.

The Perfect Wagnerite by Bernard Shaw (London, 1898; New York, 1967) and *Wagner Nights* (London, 1949) by Ernest Newman are classic introductions to the cycle. The commentary of Paul Bekker in *Richard Wagner, His Life and His Work* (trans. M. Bozman, New York, 1931, 1971) is also still exceptionally rewarding. John Culshaw has written several book about Wagner and his account of recording the Decca *Ring* cycle is of great interest to lovers of the score as well as record enthusiasts: *Ring Resounding* (London, 1967). For those interested in the staging of *The Ring*, Oswald Georg Bauer's study *Richard Wagner, The Stage Designs and Productions from the Premières to the Present* (Rizzoli, 1982) contains both accurate text and beautiful illustrations.

Contributors

Ulrich Weisstein is Professor of Comparative Literature at the University of Indiana, Bloomington.

Anthony Newcomb is Professor of Music at the University of California, Berkeley.

Derrick Puffett teaches at Wolfson College, Oxford and is a frequent contributor to English musical journals, mostly on 19th and 20th-century topics.

Andrew Porter, translator of many Verdi and Mozart operas as well as *The Ring* and *Tristan and Isolde*, is music critic of *The New Yorker*.